VOLTAIRE

CANDIDE

Clifton Robbins.

From an Old Admirer of "Cand[

Alfred Robbins
20.7.30

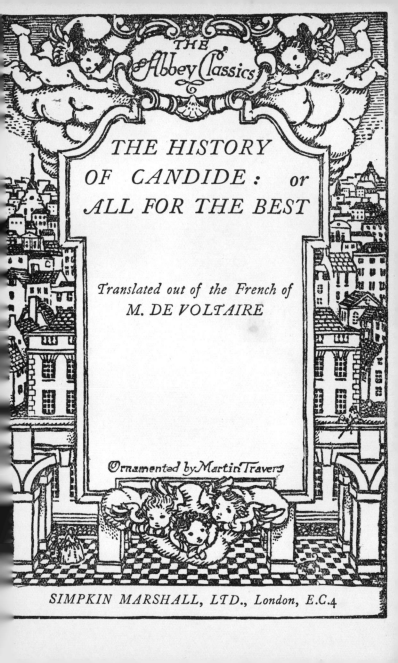

THE ABBEY CLASSICS

THE HISTORY OF CANDIDE: or ALL FOR THE BEST

Translated out of the French of
M. DE VOLTAIRE

Ornamented by Martin Travers

SIMPKIN MARSHALL, LTD., London, E.C.4

Made and Printed in Great Britain by
Hazell, Watson & Viney, Ld., London and Aylesbury.

BIOGRAPHICAL NOTE

VOLTAIRE. FRANÇOIS MARIE AROUET DE. Born 1694, the 5th son of a Parisian notary, he showed an early aptitude for literature, and despite his father's opposition, he became, while still young, associated with Vendôme's Temple coterie and also with the " court of Sceaux," the circle of the Duchesse du Maine. In consequence of a series of scurrilous lampoons on public characters of the Regency, he was exiled in 1716 and a year later was placed in the Bastile, but released after a short spell of imprisonment. The death of his father had provided him with ample means, and in addition, the Regent d'Orléans granted him a pension, notwithstanding which kindness Voltaire continued an active enemy of his patron. In 1725, as the result of a quarrel and of his receiving a public thrashing from the Chevalier de Rohan-Chabot, he was compelled to leave Paris and took refuge in England, where he remained for three years and made the acquaintance of Walpole, Bolingbroke, Congreve and Pope. On his return to France, he retired to Cirey, as the guest of Mme. du Châtelet, with whom he made his headquarters up to her death in 1749. In 1745 he was made historiographer-royal, while in 1746, the opposition to his election to the Academy, due to his attacks on religion, was overcome. In 1751, on the invitation of Frederick of Prussia, he travelled to Berlin, where he remained for the next three years, arguing, cobbling his patron's verses, and indulging his own impish humour. In 1753, in defiance of Frederick's express commands, he published *Le Diatribe du Docteur Akakia*, a satire on the views of Maupertuis, the President of the Prussian Academy of Sciences. The storm of the King's wrath broke, and Voltaire had some difficulty in making good his escape. After a short period of imprisonment at Frankfort, however, he was released and betook himself into retirement at Geneva, where his estate of Ferney became the centre of intellectual Europe. Here he remained until 1778 when he travelled to Paris in triumph, to witness the performance of his last tragedy *Iréne*. The unwonted excitement broke his health and in May, 1778, he died in his native city.

BIBLIOGRAPHICAL NOTE

The works of Voltaire comprise some 45 plays, 65 books of verse, besides a number of historical and philosophical works, romances, pamphlets, etc., and a full bibliography would therefore require a volume to itself. Below, however, are cited the more important of his writings together with a bibliographical note showing the chief editions of *Candide*.

BIBLIOGRAPHY

I.

Drama.

Oedipe. Tragedy. Published Paris : P. Ribou : 1719.

Zayre. Tragedy. First played Paris, August, 1732.
　　Published Paris : J. & B. Bauche : 1733.

La Mort de César. Tragedy. Amsterdam : 1735 (pirated edition).

La Mérope française avec quelques petites pièces de littérature. Paris : Praul fils : 1744.

Iréne. Tragedy. Played Paris, 16 March, 1778. Published Paris : 1779.

Poetry.

La Ligue ou Henri le Grand. (*La Henriade*). Geneva : Jean Mokpap : 1723.

La Pucelle d'Orlèans. Paris : 1755.

Hi$torical Works, etc.

Le Siecle de Louis XIV publiée par M. de
Francheville, conseiller aulique de Sa Maje$te
et membre de l'Académie roiale des sciences
et belle lettres de Prusse. Berlin : C. F.
Henning. 1751. 2 vols.

Hi$toire de Charles XII, roi de Suede, par M.
de V. Basle : Chr. Revis : 1731. 2 vols.

Di&ionnaire philosophique portatif. London
(Geneva) : 1764.

Romances.

Zadig, ou la De$tinée, hi$toire Orientale.
(Nancy : Leseure) : 1748.

L'Homme aux quarante écus. (Geneva) : 1768.

Candide. Vide infra.

Various.

Letters concerning the English nation by M. de
Voltaire. London : C. Davis & H. Lyon :
1733. (Lettres philosophiques).

(Diatribe du do&eur Akakia, médecin du pape—
Décret de l'Inquisition et Rapport des pro-
fesseurs de Rome as sujet d'un prétendu
president. Rome (Leyden. Luzac) : 1753.

II.

The earliest editions of *Candide* are as set out below :

(a) *Candide ou l'Optimisme, traduit de l'allemand de M. le docteur Ralph*. No imprint. (Geneva. Cramer) : 1759. 12mo. 299 pp.

(b) *Candid : or, All for the Best*. By M. de Voltaire. London : J. Nourse. 1759. 12mo. xii & 132 pp. (First English edition).

(c) *Candide*, etc. No imprint. 1761. (? Geneva). (The second part which is incontestably the work of Voltaire is herein printed for the first time.)

CONTENTS

PART I.

CONTENTS

INTRODUCTION

It is the fashion to represent *Candide* as a counterblaſt to Leibnitz. This is at once a belittlement and an irrelevance. Voltaire could no more refute Leibnitz by writing a tale than Johnson could refute Berkeley by kicking a ſtone. Leibnitz muſt be left to the metaphysicians to refute or to confirm; literature has something else and, for the world at large, something better to do. It has to delight. And *Candide*, by virtue of its delight, ſtands high among the maſterpieces of literature. It delights by the limpidity and ease of its ſtyle; by its sly wit; by its irony no less mordant though far more polite than Swift's and as sedate as Gibbon's; by its cheerfulness of temper and perfeſtion of common-sense. In one word, it delights by its Voltaireanism; for these qualities are common to all Voltairean *contes*, of which *Candide* is only the moſt famous. But it has peculiar qualities of its own. Unlike the other *contes*, it abounds in hiſtorical faſts and real personages: the Lisbon earthquake, the Jesuits of Paraguay, Admiral Byng, the six dethroned monarchs, the Robecks, the Frérons, the Trublets, celebrated French actresses and Italian singers. This gives it a "topical" interest. And it is a romance of travel, hurrying the reader from Westphalia through Bulgaria to Holland, thence via Lisbon and Cadiz to South America, with a trip to the mythical El Dorado and a return journey through Surinam to Paris, Venice and the Brenta, and finally the Levant. Best of all, it is a story of adventure : of miraculous escapes, successive disappearances and reappearances of Pangloss, Pacquette, Cacambo, Cunégonde and the young Baron of Thunder-ten-Tronckh : of kaleidoscopic changes of fortune : of autos-da-fé, galley-slaves, and diamonds as street-refuse. Indeed, you may almost be content to read *Candide*, as children read *Gulliver*, simply for the story.

Almost—for no intelligent reader of *Candide* could stop there. He could not get through a page of these adventures and marvels and catastrophes without discovering what underlies them all : a suggested argument, an intellectual appeal, a tissue of ideas. It is only superficially that the hero and his friends or foes can pass for concrete personages ; they are really abstractions

Under human traits, they are walking concepts, the passive instruments of a dialectic. And the argument of which they are the unconscious mouthpieces is one unbroken *reductio ad absurdum*. It is here that the unwary " drag in " Leibnitz. The violent contrast between Pangloss's speculative opinions (catchwords from Leibnitz) and his actual situation, so quietly presented, shakes you with laughter. If you have not refuted Leibnitz, you have at least enjoyed a ludicrous misapplication of him. Thus you get an illusion of philosophy " without tears." Amid the very ruins of Lisbon Pangloss complacently celebrates the universal reason and would console the sufferers by insisting that whatever is is right and that everything is for the best. Cacambo gravely praises the Oreillons for eating their enemies and in the same breath compliments them on their principles of public law, humanity and justice. The young Thunder-ten-Tronckh got sent back to the galleys rather than consent to his sister's marriage with one who was not a Baron of the Empire. How, asks Cunégonde of Candide, could you, " naturally so gentle," slay a Jew and a prelate in two minutes ? And Candide replies that when one is a lover, jealous and whipped by the Inquisition, one stops at nothing. Such is the Voltairean irony, bland, insinuating, a delicate repast for the literary epicure. Irony is the peculiar delight of those who are too fastidious for the emotional appeal of eloquence or the heavy touch of scholastic logic. It convinces the reason without ratiocination. This is the secret of *Candide*. It is a classic of irony.

Any lapse of the irony, a moment of emotion, would be fatal to the book. Life, Horace Walpole was fond of saying, is a comedy to those who think, a tragedy to those who feel. A *Candide* written by Rousseau, the man of feeling, would have been the most tragic of books. Voltaire piles Pelion upon Ossa in accumulating human woes and sins and savagery, and yet remains serenely comic. For he sees life always as something rational or irrational : a spectacle to act upon the brain, not to pierce the heart. Finding life, as he does, mainly irrational, he takes a mischievous delight in showing how philosophic attempts to rationalise it only add to its irrationality. It is this impish glee, this pervasive persiflage, that give the tone of the book and, incidentally, put out of court the comparison still occasionally attempted between *Candide* and its almost exact contemporary *Rasselas*. It is true that Johnson's romance, like Voltaire's, illustrates the evils of this world in a series of adventures. A work of art, however, is not to be estimated by its subject-matter, but by the spirit in which it is formed, by the reflection it gives of its author's mind ; and the serious ententiousness of Johnson is at the very opposite pole to the witty persiflage of Voltaire. *Rasselas* is by no means a negligible book. It can still be read, and, here and there, even enjoyed, but only in a moment when your *Candide* has been put away and out of mind.

The reader of taste, a little jaded perhaps by the kinematographic variety and rapidity with which the author illustrates his main thesis, will be grateful for the rare pauses in the rush. Twice, notably, Voltaire allows himself—and Candide— a brief rest : at Paris and on the Brenta. The sketch of Paris, or a side of Paris, in mid-eighteenth century, seems bitten in with acid. Candide suggested that the dark features were but shadows on a beautiful picture, but Martin replies that the shadows were horrible blots. The description of the house in the Faubourg St. Honoré, with its faro-table, its sham Marquise, its sharpers, and its boudoir adventure, reads like a disreputable chapter in the Memoirs of Casanova. Yet the true Voltairean touch is there, in a discussion of new books and a disquisition on tragedy ; and, again, at the Comédie Française, in the description of the critic who damned the play because, while the scene was in Arabia, the author didn't know a word of Arabic and, moreover, didn't believe in innate ideas. Better still, however, is the Pococurante chapter. It is a perfect antidote to the absurdities of enthusiasm. There is perverse exaggeration of course, in the virtuoso's criticisms of Homer and Virgil, Horace and Cicero, Raphael and Milton, but at the same time there is a leaven of truth ; and a vigorous bit of devil's advocacy against the classics is a refreshing change from the common conventional adulation.

And the moral of *Candide* ? The idle question cannot be avoided, for the desire for a moral seems to be inherent in all readers of stories, under the eternal delusion that literature must ever be the handmaid of ethics. Everybody at once answers, in Candide's parting word, " let us cultivate our garden." An unexceptionable moral, no doubt, but perhaps in the book a little belated. I can fancy the excellent Signor Pococurante pointing out, with a shrug, that Candide refrained from preaching this gospel until he had exhausted every form of active curiosity, encountered every kind of adventure, enjoyed every opportunity of excitement, lived the life of a globe-trotter, a millionaire and a romantic amorist—in short a life remarkably unlike that of a placid gardener.   Let us, then, by all means, contentedly cultivate our garden—but lighten our labour by an occasional dip into the exhilarating pages of *Candide*.

A. B. WALKLEY.

PART I.

CANDIDE : OR ALL FOR THE BEST

CHAPTER I

How Candide was brought up in a magnificent Castle, and how he was driuen from thence.

THERE lived in the fine castle of the Baron Thunder-ten-Tronckh, situated in Westphalia, a young man of the sweetest disposition in the world. His face was the very picture of his mind. With a good understanding, he possessed the most engaging simplicity of manners ; and, in short, was of so easy a temper, that he had got the name of Candide amongst all who knew him.

The old domestics of the household had a strong suspicion that he was the son of the

1

Baron's sister, by a very worthy gentleman in the neighbourhood, whom the lady would not however condescend to marry, because he could reckon no more than seventy-one armorial quarterings in his escutcheon, the others having been lost by the injury of time.

Monsieur, the Baron, was one of the most powerful and consequential lords in all Westphalia, for his castle had a gate to it, and even windows, and his grand saloon was hung with tapestry. Mastiffs and dogs of every degree formed a pack upon occasion to hunt with. His grooms and stable boys served for huntsmen and whippers-in ; the parson of the parish was his grand almoner. Every one called him my Lord, and every one laughed when he told his stories.

Madam, the Baroness, who weighed about three hundred weight and a half, was therefore considered as a lady of no small consequence, and gained much respect, and when she did the honors of her house, she performed the task with so much dignity that she acquired still more reverence. Mistress Cunégonde, her ladyship's daughter, was a fine rosy plump desirable girl of seventeen ; as for her brother, the Baron, son and heir, he was in every respect worthy of the stock he sprang from. Pangloss was the preceptor and the oracle of the whole family, and little Candide listened to his instructions with all the simplicity natural to his age and disposition, and believed every thing he said.

Master Pangloss taught the metaphysico-theologo-cosmolo-nigology. He could prove, to admiration, that there is no effect without a cause ; and, that in this best of all possible worlds, the baron's castle was the most magnificent of all castles, and my lady the best of all possible baronesses.

It is demonstrable, said he, that things cannot be otherwise than they are ; for as all things have been created for some end, they must necessarily be created for the best end. Observe, for instance, the nose is formed to bear spectacles, therefore we wear spectacles. The legs are visibly designed for stockings, accordingly we wear stockings. Stones were made to be hewn, and to construct castles, therefore my Lord has a magnificent castle ; for the greatest baron in the province ought to be the best lodged. Swine were created to be eaten, therefore we eat pork all the year round. It is not enough therefore to say that every thing is right, we should say every thing is in the best state it possibly could be.

Candide listened attentively, and believed implicitly ; for he thought Mistress Cunégonde excessively handsome, though he never had the courage to tell her so. He concluded, that next to the happiness of being Baron of Thunder-ten-Tronckh, the next was that of being Mistress Cunégonde, the next that of seeing her every day, and the last that of hearing the doctrine of Master Pangloss, the greatest philosopher of the whole province, and consequently of the whole world.

3

One day, when Mistress Cunégonde went to take a walk in a little neighbouring copse, which they called a park, she saw, through the bushes, the sage Doctor Pangloss giving a lecture in experimental philosophy to her mother's chambermaid, a little brown wench, very pretty, and very tractable. As Mistress Cunégonde had a great turn for the sciences, she observed all this with the utmost attention, and scarcely breathed while she beheld the experiments, which were repeated before her eyes ; she perfectly well understood the force of the doctor's reasoning upon causes and effects. She retired greatly flurried, quite pensive and filled with the desire of knowledge, imagining that she might be a very sufficient subject for philosophical experiment for young Candide, and he for her.

In her way back she happened to meet the young man ; she blushed, he blushed also : she wished him a good morning in a faultering tone ; he returned the salute, without knowing what he said. The next day, as they were rising from dinner, Cunégonde and Candide slipped behind the screen ; Miss dropped her handkerchief, the young man picked it up. She innocently took hold of his hand, and he as innocently kissed her's, with a warmth, a sensibility, a grace—all very particular ; their lips met ; their eyes sparkled ; their knees trembled ; their hands strayed.—The Baron chanced to come by ; he beholds the cause and effect, and, without hesitation, salutes Candide with some hearty kicks on the breech, and drove him out of doors. Mistress Cunégonde, the tender, the lovely Mistress Cunégonde, fainted away, and, as soon as she came to herself, the Baroness boxed her ears. Thus a general confusion was spread over this most magnificent and most agreeable of all possible castles.

CHAPTER II

What befel Candide among the Bulgarians.

THE miserable Candide, expelled like Adam from Paradise, rambled a long time without knowing where he went ; sometimes he raised his eyes, swimming in tears, towards Heaven, and sometimes he cast a melancholy look towards the magnificent castle, where dwelt the fairest of young Baronesses. He laid himself down to sleep in a furrow without the ceremony of a supper. The snow fell in great flakes, and, in the morning when he awoke, he was almost frozen to death ; however, he made shift to crawl to the next town, which was called Wald-berghoff-trarbk-dikdorff, without a penny in his pocket, and half dead with hunger and fatigue. He took up his stand at the door of an inn. He had not been long there, before two men drest in blue fixed their eyes stedfastly upon him. Faith, comrade, said one of them softly to the other, yonder is a well-made young fellow, and of just the size we want : upon which they made up to Candide, and, with the greatest civility and politeness, invited him to dine with them. Gentlemen, replied Candide, with a most engaging modesty, you do me much honour, but, upon my word, I have no money to pay my share with. Money, Sir ! said one of the blues to him, young persons of your appearance and merit never pay any thing ; why, are not you five feet five inches high ? Yes, gentlemen, that is exactly my height, replied he, with a low bow. Come then, Sir, sit down along with us ; we will not only pay your reckoning, but will never suffer such a clever young fellow as you to want money. Mankind were born to assist one another. You are perfectly right, gentlemen, said Candide, this is precisely the doctrine of Master Pangloss ; and I am convinced, by your generous behaviour, that every thing is for the best. His companions next entreat him to accept of a few crowns, which he readily complies with, at the same time offering them his note for the payment, which they refuse, and sit down to table. Don't you ardently love ? O, yes ! says Candide, I ardently love the charming Mistress Cunégonde. May be so, replied one of the blues, but that is not the question ! We ask you, whether you have not a great affection for the King of the Bulgarians ? For the King of the Bulgarians ! said Candide, oh Lord ! not at all, why, I never saw him in my life. Is it possible ! Oh, he is a most charming king ! come, we must drink his health. With all my heart, gentlemen, says Candide, and off he tosses his glass. Bravo ! cry the blues ; you are now the support, the defender, the hero of the Bulgarians ; your fortune is made ; you are in the high road to glory. So saying, they handcuff him, and carry him away to the regiment. There he is taught to wheel about to the right, to the left, to draw his rammer, to return his rammer, to present, to fire, to march, and they give him thirty blows with a cane ; the next day he performs his exercise a little better, and they give him but twenty ; the day following he comes off with ten, and is looked upon as a young fellow of surprising genius by all his comrades.

Candide was struck with amazement, and could not for the soul of him discover how he came to be a hero. One fine spring morning, he took it into his head to take a walk, and he marched strait forward, conceiving it to be a privilege of the human species, as well as of the brute creation, to make use of their legs how and when they pleased. He had not gone above two leagues, when he was overtaken by four other heroes, six feet high, who bound him neck and heels, and carried him to a dungeon. A court-martial sat upon him, and he was asked which he liked best, either to run the gantlet six and thirty times through the whole regiment, or to have his brains blown out with a dozen of musket-balls. In vain did he remonstrate to them, that the human will is free, and that he chose neither; they obliged him to make a choice, and he determined, in virtue of that divine gift, called Free Will, to run the gantlet six and thirty times. He had gone through his discipline twice, and the regiment being composed of 2000 men, they composed for him exactly 4000 strokes, which laid bare all his muscles and nerves, from the nape of his neck to his rump. As they were preparing to make him set out the third time, our young hero, unable to support it any longer, begged as a favor they would be so obliging as to blow his brains out. The favor being granted, a bandage was tied over his eyes, and he was made to kneel down. At that very instant, his Bulgarian Majesty happening to pass by, made a stop, and inquired into the delinquent's crime, and being a prince of great penetration, he found, from what he heard of Candide, that he was a young metaphysician, entirely ignorant of the world ; and therefore pardoned him with such condescension and clemency as will be celebrated in every journal, and in every age. A skilful surgeon made a cure of the flagellated Candide in three weeks, by means of emollient unguents prescribed by Dioscorides. He had scarcely recovered a little skin, and was able to walk, when the king of the Bulgarians gave battle to the king of the Abares.

CHAPTER III

How Candide escaped from the Bulgarians, and what befel him afterwards.

THOSE who have never been in battle have no conception of any thing so gallant, so well accoutred, so brilliant, and so finely disposed as the two armies. The trumpets, fifes, hautboys, drums, and cannon, formed a concert superior to any thing that was heard in hell itself. The entertainment began by a discharge of cannon, which, in the twinkling of an eye, laid flat about 6000 men on each side. The musquet carried off, out of this best of all possible worlds, nine or ten thousand scoundrels that infested its surface. The bayonet was next the sufficient reason of the deaths of several thousands. The whole might amount to 30,000 souls. Candide trembled like a philosopher, and concealed himself as well as he could during this heroic butchery.

At length, while the two kings were causing Te Deum to be sung in each of their camps, Candide took a resolution to go and reason somewhere else upon causes and effects. After passing over heaps of dead or dying men, the first place he came to was a neighbouring village, in the Arabian territories, which had been burnt to the ground by the Bulgarians, agreeable to the laws of war. Here lay a number of old men covered with wounds, who beheld their wives dying, with their throats cut, and clasping their children to their breasts all stained with blood. There several young virgins, whose bellies had been ripped open, after they had satisfied the natural appetites of the Bulgarian heroes, breathed their last ; while others, half burnt in the flames, begged to be dispatched out of the world. The ground about them was covered with the brains, arms, and legs of dead men.

Candide made all the haste he could to another village, which belonged to the Bulgarians, and there he found that the heroic Abares had acted the same tragedy. From thence continuing to walk over quivering limbs, or through ruined buildings, at length he arrived beyond the theatre of war, with a little provision in his budget, and his memory filled with the idea of his beloved Mistress Cunégonde. When he arrived in Holland his provision failed him; but having heard that the inhabitants of that country were all rich and Christians, he made himself sure of being treated by them in the same manner as at the baron's castle, before he had been driven from thence through the power of Mistress Cunégonde's bright eyes.

He asked charity of several grave looking people, who one and all answered him, that if he continued to follow this trade, they would have him sent to the house of correction, where he should be taught to get his bread. He next addressed himself to a person, who was just come from haranguing a numerous assembly for a whole hour on the subject of charity. The orator, squinting at him under his broad brimmed hat, asked him sternly, what brought him thither? and whether he was for the good old cause? Sir, said Candide, in a submissive manner, I conceive there can be no effect without a cause; every thing is necessarily concatenated and arranged for the best. It was necessary that I should be banished the presence of Mistress Cunégonde; that I should afterwards run the gantlet; and it is necessary I should beg my bread, till I am able to get it: all this could not have been otherwise. Hark ye, friend, said the orator, do you hold the pope to be antichrist? Truly, I never heard any thing about it, said Candide; but whether he is or not, I am dying for food. Thou dost not deserve to live, replied the orator, wretch, monster, that thou art! hence! avoid my sight, nor ever come near me again while thou livest. The orator's wife happened to put her head out of the window at that instant, when seeing a man, who doubted whether the pope was antichrist, she discharged upon his head a chamber pot full of——. Good heavens, to what excess does religious zeal transport the fair sex!

A man who had never been christened, an honest anabaptist, named James, was witness to the cruel and ignominious treatment showed to one of his brethren, to an unfledged Being with

C 11

a soul, and walking on two legs. Moved with pity, he carried him to his own house, caused him to be cleaned, gave him meat and drink, and made him a present of two florins, at the same time proposing to inſtruct him in his own trade of weaving Persian silks, which are fabricated in Holland. Candide, in the gratitude of his heart almoſt worship'd him, crying out, Tutor, Now I am convinced that my Pangloss told me truth, when he said that every thing was for the beſt in this world ; for your extraordinary generosity, ſtrikes me as far more natural than the inhumanity of that gentleman in the black cloak, and his wife. The next day, as Candide was walking out, he met a beggar all covered with scabs, his eyes were sunk in his head, the end of his nose eaten off, his mouth drawn on one side, his teeth as black as a coal, snuffling and coughing moſt violently, and every time he attempted to spit, out dropt a tooth.

CHAPTER IV

How Candide found his old maſter Pangloss again and what happened to them.

THE good Candide, not less affeᶜted by com-

passion than horror, immediately bestowed on
this shocking figure the two florins which the
honest anabaptist James had just before given
to him.   After gazing upon him for some time,
the miserable phantom shed tears and suddenly
threw his arms about his neck.   Candide started
back aghast ;   Alas !   said the one wretch to the
other, don't you know your dear Pangloss ?——
What do I hear ?   Is it you my dear master !
you I behold in this piteous plight ?   What
dreadful misfortune has befallen you ?   Why are
you not still in the most magnificent and delightful of all castles ?   What is become of Mistress
Cunégonde, the mirror of the fair sex, and nature's
master-piece ?   Oh Lord ! cried Pangloss, I am
so weak I cannot stand ;   upon which Candide
instantly led him to the anabaptist's table, and
procured him something to eat.   As soon as
Pangloss had a little refreshed himself, Candide
began to repeat his enquiries concerning Mistress
Cunégonde.   She is dead, replied the other.
Dead !   cried Candide, and immediately fainted
away :   his friend recovered him by the help of a
little bad vinegar, which he found by chance in
the stable.   Candide opened his eyes, and again
repeated, Dead ! is Mistress Cunégonde dead ?
Ah, where is the best of worlds now ?   But of
what illness did she die ?   Was it for grief upon
seeing her father kick me out of his magnificent
castle ?   No, replied Pangloss ;   her belly was
ripped open by the Bulgarian soldiers, after they
had ravished her as much as it was possible for

damsel to be ravished : they knocked the baron
her father on the head for attempting to defend
her ; my lady her mother was cut in pieces ;
my poor pupil was served just in the same manner
as his sister ; and as for the castle, they have not
left one stone upon another ; they have destroyed all the ducks, and the sheep, the barns,
and the trees : but we have had our revenge,
for the Abares have done the very same thing in
a neighbouring barony, which belonged to a
Bulgarian lord.

At hearing this, Candide fainted away a second
time ; but, having come to himself again, he
said all that it became him to say ; he inquired
into the cause and effect, as well as into the
sufficing reason, that had reduced Pangloss to so
miserable a condition. Alas ! replied the preceptor, it was love ; love, the comfort of the
human species ; love, the preserver of the universe, the soul of all sensible beings ; love !
tender love ! Alas, replied Candide, I have
had some knowledge of love myself, this sovereign
of hearts, this soul of our souls ; yet, it never
cost me more than a kiss, and twenty kicks on the
backside. But how could this beautiful cause
produce in you so hideous an effect ?

Pangloss made answer in these terms : O my
dear Candide, you must remember Pacquette,
that pretty wench, who waited on our noble
baroness ; in her arms I tasted the pleasures of
paradise, which produced these hell-torments
with which you see me devoured. She was

14

infected with the disease, and perhaps is since dead of it ; she received this present of a learned cordelier, who derived it from the fountain head ; he was indebted for it to an old countess, who had it of a captain of horse, who had it of a marchioness, who had it of a page ; the page had it of a jesuit, who, during his noviciate, had it in a direct line from one of the fellow-adventurers of Christopher Columbus. For my part I shall give it to no-body ; I am a dying man.

O sage Pangloss, cried Candide, what a genealogical tree have you painted, surely the devil is the root of it ? Not at all, replied the great man, it was a thing unavoidable, a necessary ingredient in the best of worlds ; for if Columbus had not caught in an island in America this disease, which contaminates the source of generation, and frequently impedes propagation itself, and is evidently opposite to the great end of nature, we should have had neither chocolate nor cochineal. It is also to be observed, that, even to the present time, in this continent of ours, this malady, like our religious controversies, is peculiar to ourselves. The Turks, the Indians, the Persians, the Chinese, the Siamese, and the Japanese are entirely unacquainted with it ; but there is a sufficing reason for them to know it in a few centuries. In the mean time, it is making prodigious havock among us, especially in those armies composed of very civil well disciplined hirelings, who determine the fate of nations ; for we may safely affirm, that, when an army of

30,000 men fights another equal in number, there are about 20,000 of them contaminated on each side.

Very surprising, indeed, said Candide, but you must get cured. Lord help me, how can I ? said Pangloss : my dear friend, I have not a penny in the world ; and you know that over the whole face of God's earth one cannot be bled, or have a blister, without a fee.

This last speech had its effect on Candide ; he flew to the charitable anabaptist James, he flung himself at his feet, and gave him so striking a picture of the miserable situation of his friend, that the good man, without any farther hesitation, agreed to take Dr. Pangloss into his house, and to pay for his cure. The cure was effected with only the loss of one eye and an ear. As he wrote a good hand, and understood accounts tolerably well, the anabaptist made him his book-keeper. At the expiration of two months, being obliged to go to Lisbon, about some mercantile affairs, he took the two philosophers with him in the same ship ; Pangloss, during the course of the voyage, explained to him how every thing was so constituted that it could not be better. James did not quite agree with him in this point : Mankind, said he, must, in some things, have deviated from their original innocence ; for they were not born wolves, and yet they worry one another like those beasts of prey. God never gave them twenty-four pounders nor bayonets, and yet they have made cannon and bayonets to destroy one another. To this account I might add, not only bankruptcies, but the law, which seizes on the effects of bankrupts, only to cheat the creditors. All this was indispensibly necessary, replied the one eyed doctor ; for private misfortunes are public benefits ; so that the more private misfortunes there are, the greater is the general good. While he was arguing in this manner, the sky was overcast, the winds blew from the four quarters of the compass, and the ship was assailed by a most terrible tempest, within sight of the port of Lisbon.

CHAPTER V

A Tempest, a Shipwreck, an Earthquake ; and what else befel Dr. Pangloss, Candide, and James the Anabaptist.

THE horrible sickness occasioned by the rolling of the vessel, which tears the human frame almost to pieces, took from one half of the passengers all sense of danger ; the other half screamed and prayed alternately. The sails were torn to pieces, the masts were carried away, and the vessel half full of water, in short she was a compleat wreck.— 'Twas in vain to pretend to assist, for no one could

17

give orders or be heard. The anabaptist gave what assistance he could, and remained upon the deck, when a brutal sailor knocked him down ; but, with the violence of the blow, the tar himself tumbled head foremost over-board, and fell upon a piece of the broken mast, which he immediately grasped. Honest James, forgetting the injury he had so lately received from him, flew to his assistance, and, with great difficulty, hauled him in again, but, in the attempt, was, by a sudden jerk of the ship, thrown over-board himself, in sight of the very fellow whom he had risked his life to save, and who took not the least notice of him in this distress. Candide, who beheld all that past, and saw his benefactor one moment rising above water, and the next swallowed up by the merciless waves, was preparing to jump after him ; but was prevented by the philosopher Pangloss, who demonstrated to him, that the coast of Lisbon had been made on purpose for the anabaptist to be drowned there. While he was proving his argument *a priori*, the ship foundered, and the whole crew perished, except Pangloss, Candide, and the ungrateful sailor who had been the means of drowning the good ana-baptist. The villain swam ashore ; but Pangloss and Candide got to land upon a plank.

As soon as they had recovered themselves from their surprize and fatigue, they walked towards Lisbon ; with what little money they had left, they thought to save themselves from starving, after having escaped drowning.

Scarce had they done lamenting the loss of their benefactor, and set foot in the city, when they perceived the earth to tremble under their feet, and the sea, swelling and foaming in the harbour, dash in pieces the vessels that were riding at anchor. Large sheets of flames and cinders covered the streets and public places ; the houses tottered, and were tumbled topsy-turvy, even to their foundations, which were themselves destroyed, and thirty thousand inhabitants of both sexes, young and old, were buried beneath the ruins. The sailor, whistling and swearing, cried, Damn it, there's something to be got here. What can be the sufficing reason of this phenomenon ? said Pangloss. It is certainly the day of judgment, said Candide. The sailor, defying death in the pursuit of plunder, rushed into the midst of the ruin, where he found some money, with which he got drunk, and, after he had slept himself sober, he purchased the favours of the first good-natured wench that came in his way, amidst the ruins of demolished houses, and the groans of half-buried and expiring persons. Pangloss pulled him by the sleeve : Friend, said he, this is not right, you trespass against the universal reason, and have mistaken your time. Death and ounds ! answered the other, I am a sailor, and born at Batavia, and have trampled four times upon the crucifix in as many voyages to Japan : you are come to a good hand with your universal reason.

In the mean time, Candide, who had been

wounded by some pieces of stone that fell from the houses, lay stretched in the street, almost covered with rubbish : For God's sake, said he to Pangloss, get me a little wine and oil, I am dying. This concussion of the earth is no new thing, replied Pangloss, with the most unfeeling coolness, the city of Lima, in America, experienced the same last year ; the same cause, the same effects : there is certainly a train of sulphur all the way under ground from Lima to Lisbon. It may be so, for nothing is more probable, said Candide ; but, for the love of God, a little oil and wine. Probable ! replied the philosopher, I maintain that the thing is demonstrable : Candide fainted away, and Pangloss fetched him some water from a neighbouring spring.

The next day, having found some eatables among the ruins, they repaired their exhausted strength. After this, they assisted the inhabitants in relieving the distressed and wounded who had been so happy as to escape with their lives. Some, whom they had humanely assisted, gave them as good a dinner as could be expected under such terrible circumstances. The repast, indeed, was mournful, and the company moistened their bread with their tears ; but Pangloss endeavoured to comfort them under this affliction, by affirming, that things could not be otherwise than they were : for, said he, all this is for the very best end ; for if there is a volcano at Lisbon, it could be on no other spot ; for it is impossible but things should be as they are, for every thing is for the best.

By the side of the preceptor sat a little man dressed in black, who was one of the familiars of the inquisition. This person, taking him up with great complaisance, said, possibly, my good Sir, you do not believe in original sin ; for if every thing is best, there could have been no such thing as the fall or punishment of men.

I humbly ask your excellency's pardon, answered Pangloss, still more politely ; for the fall of man, and the curse consequent thereupon, necessarily entered into the system of the best of worlds. That is as much as to say, Sir, rejoined the familiar, you do not believe in free-will. Your excellency will be so good as to excuse me, said Pangloss, free-will is consistent with absolute necessity ; for it was necessary we should be free, for in that the will———

Pangloss was in the midst of his proposition, when the inquisitor made a private sign to the attendant, who was helping him to a glass of Port wine.

CHAPTER VI

How the Portuguese made a superb Auto-da-fe to prevent any future Earthquakes, and how Candide underwent public Flagellation.

As soon as the earthquake was over, some wise men took it into their heads that nothing would so effectually prevent the return of such a calamity in the kingdom as to present the inhabitants with a grand Auto-da-fe, it having been decided by the university of Coimbra, that the burning a few people alive by a slow fire, and with great ceremony, is an infallible secret to prevent earthquakes.

In consequence thereof, they had seized on a Biscayner for marrying his godmother, and on two Portuguese for taking out the bacon of a larded pullet they were eating; after dinner, they came and secured Dr. Pangloss, and his pupil Candide ; the one for speaking his mind, and the other for having listened to him, (as indeed he always did) with great attention, and seeming to approve what he had said. They were conducted to separate apartments, extremely cool, where they were never incommoded with the sun. Eight days afterwards they were each dressed in a san-benito, and their heads were adorned with paper mitres. The mitre and san-benito worn by Candide, were painted with flames reversed, and with devils that had neither tails nor claws ; but Dr. Pangloss' devils had both tails and claws, and his flames were upright. In these habits they marched in procession, and heard a very pathetic sermon, which was followed by an anthem, accompanied by very fine music and very much out of tune. Candide was flogged in regular cadence, while the anthem was singing ; the Biscayner, and the two men who would not eat bacon, were burnt, and Pangloss was hanged, which is not a common custom at these solemnities. The same day there was another earthquake, which made most dreadful havock.

Candide, amazed, terrified, confounded, astonished, all bloody, and trembling from head to foot, said to himself, If this is the best of all possible worlds, what are all the rest ? As to myself if I had only been whipped, I could have put up with it, as I did among the Bulgarians ; but, oh, my dear Pangloss ! my beloved master ! thou greatest of philosophers ! that ever I should live to see thee hanged, without knowing for what ! O my dear anabaptist, thou best of men, that it should be thy fate to be drowned in the very harbour ! O Mistress Cunégonde, pearl of young ladies ! that it should be your fate to have your belly ript open.

He was making the best of his way from the place where he had been preached to, whipt, absolved, and received benediction, when he

was accosted by an old woman, who said to him,
Take courage, child, and follow me.

CHAPTER VII

*How the Old Woman took care of Candide, and how
he found the Object of his Love.*

CANDIDE could not for the soul of him take
courage after such complicated terrors, and such
a severe flogging ; however he followed the old
woman to a decayed house, where she gave him
a pot of pomatum to anoint his sores, showed him
a very neat bed, with a suit of clothes hanging up
by it ; and set victuals and drink before him.
There, said she, eat, drink, and sleep, and may
our blessed lady of Atocha, and the great St.
Anthony of Padua, and the illustrious St. James
of Compostella, take you under their protection.
I shall be back to-morrow. Candide, struck with
amazement at what he had seen, at what he had
suffered, and still more with the charity of the old
woman, would have shewn his acknowledgment
by kissing her hand. It is not my hand you
ought to kiss, said the old woman, I shall be back
to-morrow. Anoint your back, eat, and take
your rest. Sleep, that balmy friend to human

nature, visited the eyes of the wretched Candide notwithstanding all he had suffered : in short he supt heartily upon the provision the old woman left him, and fell asleep. The next morning the old woman brought him his breakfast ; examined his back, and rubbed it herself with another ointment. She returned at the proper time, and brought him his dinner ; and at night she visited him again with his supper. The next day she observed the same ceremonies. All this was kindly carried on in dumb shew, to the great surprise of Candide. Who are you ? said Candide to her ; What God has inspired you with so much goodness ? What return can I make you for this charitable assistance ? The good old Beldame kept a profound silence. In the evening she returned, but without his supper ; Come along with me, said she, but do not speak a word. She took him under her arm, and walked with him about a quarter of a mile into the country, till they came to a lonely house, surrounded with moats and gardens. The old woman knocked at a little door, which was immediately opened, and she showed him up a pair of back stairs, into a small closet richly adorned with gilding. There she made him sit down on a brocaded sofa, shut the door upon him, and left him. Candide thought himself in a dream, and that his past life had been a very horrible dream, and his present situation a very pleasant one.

The old woman soon returned, supporting with great difficulty a young lady, who trembled exceedingly. She was of a majestic mien and stature ; her dress was rich, and glittering with diamonds, and her face was covered with a veil. Take off that veil, said the old woman to Candide. The young man approaches, and, with a trembling hand, takes off her veil. What a happy moment ! What surprise ! he thought he beheld Mistress Cunégonde ; he did behold her, it was she herself. His strength fails him, he cannot utter a word, he falls at her feet. Cunégonde falls back upon the sofa. The old woman bedews them with spirits ; they recover, they begin to speak. At first they could express themselves only in broken accents ; their questions and answers were alternately interrupted with sighs, tears, and exclamations. The old woman desired them to make as little noise as possible ; and after this prudent admonition left them together. Good heavens ! cried Candide, is it you ? Is it Mistress Cunégonde I behold, and alive ? Do I find you again in Portugal ? then you have not been ravished ! they did not rip open your belly, as the philosopher Pangloss informed me ! Indeed but they did, replied Mistress Cunégonde ? but these two accidents do not always prove mortal. But were your father and mother killed ? Alas ! answered she, it is but too true ! and she wept. And your brother ? And my brother also. And how came you into Portugal ? And how did you know of my being here ? And by what strange adventure did you contrive to have me brought into this house ? And how——I will tell you all, replied the lady, but first you must acquaint me with all that has befallen you, since the innocent kiss you gave me, and the rude kicking you received in consequence of it.

Candide, with the greatest respect, prepared to obey the commands of his fair mistress, and though he was in great surprise and confusion, though his voice was low and tremulous, though his back pained him, yet he gave her a most ingenuous account of every thing that had befallen him since the moment of their separation. Cunégonde, with her eyes uplifted to heaven, shed tears when he related the death of the good anabaptist James, and of Pangloss ; after which, she thus related her adventures to Candide, who lost not one syllable she uttered, and seemed to devour her with his eyes all the time she was speaking.

CHAPTER VIII

The History of Cunégonde.

It pleased Heaven in its anger to send the Bulgarian soldiers to our fine castle of Thunder-ten-Tronckh, in the midst of the night, when I was in a profound sleep. My father and mother were soon butchered, as well as my poor brother. As for me, a strapping Bulgarian soldier, six feet high, perceiving that I had fainted away at this sight, attempted to ravish me ; the operation brought me to my senses. I cried, I struggled, I bit, I scratched, I would have torn the tall Bulgarian's eyes out, not knowing that what had happened at my father's castle was a customary thing. The brutal soldier, enraged at my resistance, gave me a cut in the left side with his hanger, the mark of which I still carry. I hope I shall see it, said Candide, with all imaginable simplicity. You shall, said Cunégonde ; but let me proceed. Pray do, replied Candide. She went on with the story.

A Bulgarian captain coming in, saw me weltering in my blood, and the soldier continuing his operation as if no one had been present. The officer, enraged at the fellow's want of respect to him, killed him upon my body. This captain took care of me, had my wounds dressed, and carried me prisoner of war to his quarters. I washed what little linen he was master of, and cooked his dinner for him : he certainly found me very witty and seemed extremely fond of me ; neither can I deny that he was well made, and had a white soft skin, but he was very stupid, and knew nothing of philosophy : it might plainly be perceived that he had not been educated under Doctor Pangloss. In three months time, having lost all his money at play, and being grown tired of me, he sold me to a Jew, named Don Issachar, who traded to Holland and Portugal, and was passionately fond of women. This Jew shewed me great kindness, in hopes to gain my favours ; but he never could succeed. I resisted his attacks more successfully than I did those of the Bulgarian soldier. A modest woman may be ravished once ; but her virtue is the stronger for it. In order to bring me to his lure by degrees, he brought me to this country house you now see. I had hitherto believed that nothing could equal the beauty of the castle of Thunder-ten-Tronckh ; but I have been undeceived.

The grand inquisitor saw me one day at mass, ogled me all the time of service, and, when it was over, sent to let me know he wanted to speak with me about some private business. I was conducted to his palace, where I told him all my story : he represented to me how much it was beneath a person of my birth to belong to a circumcised Israelite. He caused a proposal to be made to Don Issachar, that he should resign me to his lordship. Don Issachar, being the court banker, and a man of some consequence, did not chuse to acquiesce. His lordship threatened him with an Auto-da-fé ; in short, my Jew was frightened into a composition, and it was agreed between them, that the house and myself should belong to both in common ; that the Jew should have Monday, Wednesday, and the Sabbath to himself ; and the inquisitor the other four days of the week. This agreement has subsisted almost six months ; but not without several contests, whether the space from Saturday night to Sunday morning belonged to the old or the new law. For my part, I have hitherto withstood them both, and truly I believe this is the very reason why they are both so fond of me.

At length, to get rid of the scourge of earthquakes, and to intimidate Don Issachar, my lord inquisitor was pleased to celebrate an Auto-dafé. He did me the honour to invite me to the ceremony. I had a very good seat ; and refreshments of all kinds were offered the ladies between mass and the execution. I was dreadfully shocked at the burning the two Jews, and the honest Biscayner, who married his godmother ; but how great was my surprise, my consternation, and concern, when I beheld a figure so like Pangloss, dressed in a san-benito and mitre ! I rubbed my eyes, I looked at him attentively. I saw him hanged, and I fainted away : scarce had I recovered my senses, when I beheld you stark-naked ; this was the height of horror, grief, and despair. I must confess to you for a truth, that your skin is far whiter and more blooming, than that of the Bulgarian captain. This spectacle worked me up to a pitch of distraction. I screamed out, and would have said, Hold, barbarians ! but my voice failed me ; and indeed my cries would have signified nothing. After you had been severely whipped how is it possible, said I to myself, that the lovely Candide and the sage Pangloss should be a

Lisbon, the one to receive an hundred lashes, and the other to be hanged, by order of my lord inquisitor, of whom I am so great a favourite ? Pangloss deceived me moſt cruelly, in saying that every thing is for the beſt in this world of ours.

What a ſtate was I in, thus agitated and perplexed ! now diſtraĉted and loſt, now half dead with grief, my whole brain was full of the murder of my father, mother, and brother, committed before my eyes ; the insolence of the rascally Bulgarian soldier ; the cruel wound he gave me ; my servitude ; my being a cook wench to my Bulgarian captain ; my subjeĉtion to a rascally Jew, and my cruel inquisitor ; the hanging of Doĉtor Pangloss ; the *Miserere* sung while you were whipt ; and particularly the kiss I gave you behind the screen, the laſt day I ever beheld you. I returned thanks to God for having brought you to the place where I was after so many trials. I charged the old woman who attends me, to bring you hither, as soon as was convenient. She has punĉtually executed my orders, and I now enjoy the inexpressible satisfaĉtion of seeing you, hearing you, and speaking to you. But you muſt certainly be half dead with hunger ; I myself have a great inclination to eat, and so let us sit down to supper.

Upon this the two lovers immediately placed themselves at table, and, after having supped, they returned to seat themselves again on the magnificent sofa already mentioned, where they were in amorous dalliance, when Signor Don Issachar, whose turn it was to be master of the house, entered unexpectedly ; it was the Sabbath day, and he came to enjoy his privilege, and sigh forth his passion at the feet of the fair Cunégonde.

CHAPTER IX

What happened to Cunégonde, Candide, the grand Inquisitor, and the Jew.

THIS Issachar was the most passionate little Hebrew that had ever been in Israel, since the captivity of Babylon. What then, said he, thou Gallilean B—h ? is not the inquisitor enough for thee, but this rascal must come in for a share with me ? In uttering these words, he drew out a long poniard, which he always carried about him, and never dreaming that his adversary had any arms, he flew at Candide like a tyger ; but our honest Westphalian had received a handsome sword of the old woman with the suit of cloaths. Candide draws his rapier ; and though he was the most gentle, sweet tempered young man breathing, he whips it into the Israelite, and laid him sprawling on the floor at the fair Cunégonde's feet.

Holy Virgin ! cried she, what will become of us ? A man killed in my apartment ! If the peace-officers come, we are undone. Had not Pangloss been hanged, replied Candide, he would have given us most excellent advice in this emergency, for he was a very deep philosopher. But, since he is not here, let us consult the old woman. She was a very sagacious old lady, and was beginning to give her advice, when another little door opened on a sudden. It was now one o'clock in the morning, and of course the beginning of Sunday, which, according to stipulation belonged to my lord inquisitor. Entering the apartment, he discovers the flagellated Candide with his drawn sword in his hand, a dead body stretched on the floor, Cunégonde frightened out of her wits, and the old woman giving advice.

Now what passed in Candide's head at this critical moment was exactly this, if this holy man, thought he, should call assistance, I shall most undoubtedly be burnt alive, and Mistress Cunégonde may perhaps keep me company ; besides, he was the cause of my being so cruelly whipped ; he is my rival ; and besides I have now begun to dip my hands in blood, and there is no time for deliberation. This whole train of reasoning was clear and instantaneous ; so that, without giving time to the inquisitor to recover from his surprise, he ran him through the body, and laid him by the side of the Jew. Good God ! cries Cunégonde, here's another fine piece of work ! now there can be no mercy for us, we are excommunicated to all the devils in hell ; our laſt hour is come. But how in the name of wonder could you, who are of the mildeſt temper in the world, dispatch a Jew and a Prieſt in two minutes time ? Beautiful miſtress, answered Candide, when a man is in love, is jealous, and has been flogged by the inquisition, he becomes loſt to all reflection.

The old woman then thought it high time to speak ; there are three Andalusian horses in the ſtable, said she, with as many bridles and saddles ; let the brave Candide get them ready ; madam has a parcel of moidores and jewels ; let us mount immediately, though I have only one buttock to sit upon ; let us set out for Cadiz ; it is the fineſt weather in the world, and there is great pleasure in travelling in the cool of the night.

Candide, without any farther hesitation, saddles the three horses ; and Miſtress Cunégonde, the old woman, and he, set out, and travelled thirty miles without once baiting. While they were making the beſt of their way, the holy Brotherhood enter the house. My Lord the Inquisitor is interred in a magnificent manner, and Mr. Issachar's body is thrown upon a dunghill.

Candide, Cunégonde, and the old woman, had, by this time, reached the little town of Avacena, in the midſt of the mountains of Sierra Morena, and the following conversation ensued in an inn, where they had taken up their quarters.

CHAPTER X

In what distress Candide, Cunégonde, and the Old Woman arrive at Cadiz; and of their Embarkation.

BLESS me, cries Mistress Cunégonde, bursting into tears, who can have robbed me of my moidores and jewels ? how shall we subsist ? What shall we do ? Where shall I find inquisitors and Jews to supply me with more ? Alas ! said the old woman, I have a shrewd suspicion of a reverend father Cordelier, who lay last night in the same inn with us at Badajoz : God forbid I should form a rash judgment, but he came into our room twice, and he set off in the morning long before us. Alas ! said Candide, Pangloss has often demonstrated to me that the goods of this world are common to all men, and that every one has an equal right to the enjoyment of them ; but even according to these principles, the Cordelier ought to have left us enough to carry us to the end of our journey. Have you nothing at all left, my dear Mistress Cunégonde ? Not a stiver replied she. What is to be done then ? said Candide. Sell one of the horses, replied the old woman, I will get behind Mistress Cunégonde, though I have only one buttock to ride on, and we shall reach Cadiz, never fear.

In the same inn there was a Benedictine Friar who piously took this advantage of their necessities, and bought the horse very cheap. Candide, Cunégonde, and the old woman, after passing through Lucina, Chellas, and Letriza, arrived at length at Cadiz. A fleet was then getting ready, and troops were assembling in order to reduce the reverend fathers the Jesuits of Paraguay to order, who were accused of having excited one of the Indian tribes in the neighbourhood of the town of the holy Sacrament to revolt against the kings of Spain and Portugal. Candide, having been in the Bulgarian service, performed the military exercise of that nation, before the General of this little army, with so intrepid an air, and with such agility and expedition, that he gave him the command of a company of foot. Being now made a Captain, he embarks with Mistress Cunégonde, the old woman, two valets, and the two Andalusian horses, which had once belonged to the stable of the Grand Inquisitor of Portugal.

During their voyage, they amused themselves with many profound reasonings on poor Pangloss's philosophy. We are now going into another world, and surely it must be there that every thing is best ; for I must confess, that what passes in ours is enough to make one's heart ache, both as to the physical and moral part. Though certainly I love you most truly, said Mistress Cunégonde, yet I still shudder at the reflection of what I have seen and experienced. All will be well, replied Candide, the sea of this new world is

already better than our European seas : it is
smoother, and the winds blow more regularly.
God grant it, said Cunégonde ; but I have met
with such terrible treatment in this, that I have
almost lost all hopes of a better.   What murmuring and complaining you make ! cried the old
woman : if you had suffered half what I have
done, there might be some reason for it.   Mistress
Cunégonde could scarce refrain laughing at the
good old woman, and thought it droll enough
to pretend to a greater share of misfortunes than
herself.   Alas ! my good dame, said she, unless
you have been ravished by two Bulgarians, had
received two deep wounds in your belly, had seen
two of your own castles demolished, had lost two
fathers and two mothers, and seen both of them
barbarously murdered before your eyes, and, to
sum up all, had two lovers whipt at an Auto-
da-fé, I cannot see how you could be more unfortunate than I am.   Add to this, though born
a baroness, and bearing seventy-two quarterings,
I have been reduced to a cook-wench.   Mistress,
replied the old woman, you know nothing of my
family as yet ; if I was to show you my backside,
you would not talk in this manner, but suspend
your judgment. This speech raised a high
curiosity in Candide and Cunégonde ; and the
old woman went on as follows.

CHAPTER XI

The History of the Old Woman.

My eyes were not always so red and sore as you now see them. My nose did not always touch my chin, nor was I always a servant. You muſt know that I am the daughter of Pope Urban X, by the Princess of Paleſtrina. 'Till the age of fourteen I was brought up in a caſtle, to which all the caſtles of the German Barons would not have been fit for ſtabling, and so coſtly was my dress that one of my robes was of more value than half the province of Weſtphalia. I grew up, and improved in beauty, in wit, and in every graceful accomplishment, in the midſt of pleasures, homage, and the higheſt expeſtations. I already began to be the Idol of the men : my breaſt began to display its charms ; and such a breaſt ! white, firm, and formed like that of Venus of Medicis : my eye-brows were as black as jet ; and as for my eyes, they darted flames, and eclipsed the luſtre of the ſtars, as I was told by the poets of our part of the world. My women who waited on me were in extasies when they dressed and undressed me, and saw me before and behind ; and all the men longed to be in their places.

I was contraſted to a sovereign prince of Massa Carara. Such a prince ! as handsome as myself, sweet-tempered, agreeable, witty, and in love with me to distraction. I loved him too, as most people do their first love, with rapture, transport, and idolatry. The nuptials were prepared with surprising pomp and magnificence ; the ceremony was attended with feasts, carousals, and burlettas : all Italy composed sonnets in my praise, not one of which was tolerable. I was on the point of reaching the summit of bliss, when an old Marchioness, who had been mistress to the Prince my husband, invited him to drink chocolate. In less than two hours after he returned from the visit he died in most terrible convulsions : but this is a mere trifle. My mother, distracted to the highest degree, and yet less afflicted than I was, determined to absent herself for some time from so fatal a place. As she had a very fine estate in the neighbourhood of Gaieta, we embarked on board a galley, which was gilded like the high altar of St. Peter's at Rome. In our passage we were boarded by a Sallee Rover. Our men defended themselves like true Pope's soldiers ; they flung themselves upon their knees, laid down their arms, and begged the corsair to give them absolution in *articulo mortis.*

The Moors presently stripped us as bare as ever we were born. My mother, my maids of honour, and myself, were served all in the same manner. It is amazing how expert these gentry are at undressing people. But what surprised me most was, that they thrust their fingers into that part of our bodies where we women seldom admit any thing but——to enter. I thought it a very strange kind of ceremony ; but we are apt to think every thing strange when we have seen but little of the world. I afterwards learnt, that it was to discover if we had no diamonds concealed. This practice has been established time immemorial among those humane and civilized nations that scour the seas. I was informed, that the religious knights of Malta never fail to make this search, whenever any Moors of either sex fall into their hands. It is a part of the law of nations, from which they never deviate.

You may easily conceive how great a hardship it was for a young princess and her mother to be made slaves, and carried to Morocco. You may likewise imagine, what we must have suffered on board a corsair. My mother was still extremely handsome, our maids of honour, and even our common waiting women, had more charms than were to be found in all Africa. As to myself, I was enchanting ; I was beauty itself, and was a maid. But, alas ! I did not remain so long ; this precious flower, which was reserved for the lovely prince of Massa Carara, was cropt by the Captain of the Moorish vessel, who was a hideous negro, and even thought he did me infinite honour. Indeed, both the Princess of Palestrina and myself must have had very strong constitutions to undergo all the hardships and violences we suffered till our arrival at Morocco.

But I will not detain you any longer with such common things, they are hardly worth mentioning.

Upon our arrival at Morocco, we found that kingdom deluged in blood. Fifty sons of the Emperor Muley Ishmael were each at the head of a party. This produced fifty civil wars of blacks against blacks, of tawnies against tawnies, and of mulattoes against mulattoes. In short, the whole empire was one continued scene of carnage.

As soon as we landed, a party of blacks, of a contrary party to that of my captain, came to rob him of his booty. Next to the money and jewels, we were the most valuable things he had. I was witness on this occasion to such a battle as you never beheld in your cold European climates. The northern nations have not that fermentation in their blood, nor that raging lust for women that is so common in Africa. The natives of Europe seem to have their veins filled with milk only ; but fire and vitriol circulate in those of the inhabitants of Mount Atlas, and the neighbouring provinces. They fought with the fury of the lions, tigers, and serpents of their country, to know who should have us. A Moor seized my mother by the right arm, while my captain's lieutenant held her by the left ; another Moor laid hold of her by the right leg, and one of our corsairs held her by the other. In this manner were almost every one of our women dragged between four soldiers. My captain kept me concealed behind him, and with his drawn scymetar cut down every one who opposed him ; at length I saw all our Italian women and my mother, mangled and torn in pieces by the monsters who contended for them. The captives, my companions, the Moors who took us, the soldiers, the sailors, the blacks, the whites, the mulattoes, and lastly, my captain himself, were all slain, and I remained alone fainting and almost dead upon a heap of carcases. The like barbarous scenes were transacted every day over the whole country, which is an extent of three hundred leagues, and yet they never missed the five stated times of prayer enjoined by their prophet Mahomet.

I disengaged myself with great difficulty from such a heap of slaughtered bodies, and made a shift to crawl to a large orange tree that stood on the bank of a neighbouring rivulet, where I fell down exhausted with fatigue, and overwhelmed with horror, despair, and hunger. My senses being overpowered, I fell asleep, or rather seemed to be in a trance from the exhausted state I was in. Thus I lay in a state of weakness and insensibility, between life and death, when I felt myself pressed by something that moved up and down upon my body. This brought me to myself ; I opened my eyes, and saw a fair complexioned man, who sighed and muttered these words between his teeth, *O che sciagura d'essere senza coglioni !*

CHAPTER XII

The Adventures of the Old Woman continued.

I was equally pleased and aſtonished to hear the sound of my own language, and not less surprized at the young man's lamentation. I told him that there were many heavier misfortunes in the world than what he complained of. And to convince him of it, I gave him a short hiſtory of the horrible disaſters that had befallen me ; and, as soon as I had finished, fell into a swoon again. He carried me in his arms to a neighbouring cottage, where he had me put to bed, procured me something to eat, waited on me with the greateſt attention, comforted me, caressed me, told me that he had never seen any thing so beautiful as myself, and that he had never before so much regretted the loss of what no one could reſtore to him. I had the misfortune (said he) to be born at Naples, where they caponise two or three thousand children every year : some of them die of the operation, but others acquire by that means voices far beyond the moſt tuneful of your ladies ; and others are sent to govern ſtates and empires. I underwent this operation very happily, and was one of the singers in the Princess of Paleſtrina's chapel. How, cried I, in my mother's chapel ! The Princess of Pale-

E

ſtrina your mother, cried he, burſting into a flood of tears ! is it possible you should be the beautiful young princess whom I had the care of bringing up till she was six years old, and who, at that tender age, promised to be as fair as I now behold you ? I am the same, replied I. My mother lies about a hundred yards from hence, cut in pieces, and buried under a heap of dead bodies.

I then related to him all that had happened to me, and he in return recited all his adventures. and how he had been sent to the court of the Emperor of Morocco by a Chriſtian prince, to conclude a treaty with that monarch ; in which it was agreed that the Moorish King was to be furnished with military ſtores, and ships to enable him to deſtroy the commerce of other Chriſtian governments. I have executed my commission said the eunuch ; I am going to take shipping at Ceuta, and I'll take you along with me to Italy *Ma che sciagura d'essere senza coglioni !*

I thanked him with tears of joy, but inſtead o taking me with him into Italy, he very kindl carried me to Algiers, and sold me to the dey o that province. I had not been long a slave, whe the plague, which had made the tour of Afric Asia, and Europe, broke out at Algiers with re doubled fury. You have seen an earthquake but tell me, Miſtress, had you ever the plague Never, answered the young baroness.

Well then, said the old woman, I can assur you that an earthquake is a trifle to it. It is ver common in Africa : I was seized with it. Figure to yourself the distressed situation of the daughter of a pope, only fifteen years old, and who in less than three months had felt the miseries of poverty and slavery ; had been ravished almost every day ; had beheld her mother cut into four quarters ; had experienced all the miseries of famine and war, and was now dying of the plague at Algiers. I did not, however, die of it ; but my eunuch, and the dey, and almost the whole seraglio of Algiers, were swept off.

As soon as the first fury of this dreadful pestilence was over, a sale was made of the dey's slaves. I was purchased by a merchant, who carried me to Tunis. This man sold me to another merchant, who sold me again to another at Tripoli ; from Tripoli I was sold to Alexandria, from Alexandria to Smyrna, and from Smyrna to Constantinople. After many changes, I at length became the property of an aga of the Janissaries, who, soon after I came into his possession, was ordered away to the defence of Asoph, then besieged by the Russians.

The aga, who was a man of splendor and intrigue, took his whole seraglio with him, and lodged us in a small fort, with two black eunuchs and twenty soldiers upon the Palus Moetis for our guard. Our army made a great slaughter among the Russians, but they soon returned us the compliment. Asoph was taken by storm, and the enemy spared neither age, sex, nor condition, but put all to the sword, and laid the city

45

in ashes. Our little fort alone held out ; they resolved to reduce us by famine. The twenty janissaries who were left to defend it, had bound themselves by an oath never to surrender the place. Being reduced to the extremity of famine, they found themselves obliged to kill our two eunuchs, and eat them rather than violate their oath. But this horrible repast soon failed them, they next determined to support the remains of life by devouring the women.

We had a very pious and humane iman, who made them a most excellent sermon on this occasion, exhorting them not to kill us all at once, Only cut off one of the buttocks of each of those ladies, said he, and you will find an excellent meal ; if ye are still under the necessity of having recourse to the same expedient again, the fellow to it will supply you a few days hence. Heaven will approve of so charitable an action and work your deliverance.

By the force of this eloquence he easily persuaded them, and all underwent this inhuman amputation. The iman applied the same balsam as they do to children after circumcision. We were all at death's door from the operation.

The Janissaries had scarcely time to finish the repast with which we had supplied them, when the Russians attacked the place by means of flat-bottomed boats, and not a single janissary escaped. The Russians paid no regard to the condition we were in ; but as there are French surgeons in all parts of the world, a skilful operator took us under his care, and made a cure of us; and I shall never forget, while I live, that as soon as my wounds were perfectly healed, he made me certain proposals of an amorous nature. In general, he desired us all to have a good heart, assuring us that the like had happened in many sieges ; and that it was perfectly agreeable to the laws of war.

As soon as my companions were in a condition to walk, they were sent to Moscow. As for me, I fell to the lot of a Boyard, who put me to work in his garden, and gave me twenty lashes a-day. But this nobleman having, in about two years afterwards, been broke alive upon the wheel, with about thirty others, for some court intrigues, I took advantage of the event, and made my escape. I travelled over a great part of Russia. I was a long time an inn-keeper's servant at Riga, then at Rostock, Wisinar, Leipsick, Cassel, Utrecht, Leyden, the Hague, and Rotterdam : I have grown old in misery and disgrace, living with only half my backside, and in the perpetual remembrance that I was a pope's daughter. I have been an hundred times upon the point of killing myself, but still was fond of life. This ridiculous weakness is, perhaps, one of the dangerous principles implanted in our nature. For what can be more absurd than to persist in carrying a burden of which we wish to be eased ? to detest, and yet to strive to preserve our existence ? In a word, to caress the serpent that devours us, and hug him close to our bosoms till he had gnawed into our hearts ?

In the different countries which it has been my fate to traverse, and the many inns where I have been a servant, I have observed a prodigious number of people who held their existence in abhorrence, and yet I never knew more than twelve who voluntarily put an end to their misery ; namely, three Negroes, four Englishmen, as many Genoese, and a German professor, named Robek. My last place was with the Jew, Don Issachar, who placed me near your person, my fair lady ; to whose fortunes I have attached myself, and have been more affected by your miseries than my own. I should never have even mentioned mine to you, had you not a little piqued me on the subject of sufferings ; and if it had not been to tell stories on board a ship in order to pass away the time. In short, my dear Mistress, I have acquired a great deal of knowledge and experience in the world, therefore take my advice ; strive to divert yourself, and prevail upon each passenger to tell his story, and if there is one of them all that has not cursed his existence many times, and said to himself over and over again, that he was the most wretched of mortals, I give you leave to throw me head foremost into the sea.

CHAPTER XIII

*How Candide was obliged to leave the fair Cuné-
gonde and the Old Woman.*

THE beautiful Cunégonde having been thus informed of the old woman's adventures and rank
in life, paid her all the respect that was due to a
pope's daughter ; she closed with her proposition, and prevailed on the passengers to relate
their adventures in their turns, and was at length,
as well as Candide, compelled to acknowledge
that the old woman was in the right. It is a
thousand pities, said Candide, that the sage
Pangloss was hanged, contrary to the custom of an
Auto-da-fé, for he would have read us a most
admirable lecture on the moral and physical evils
which overspread the earth and sea ; and I think
from what I have experienced I should have
courage enough to presume to offer (with all due
respect) some few objections.

Whilst each passenger was giving the history
of his life, the ship was advancing to its post of
destination, and at length arrived at Buenos
Ayres, where Cunégonde, Captain Candide, and
the old woman, landed, and went to wait upon the
Governor Don Fernando d'Ibaraa, y Figueora,
y Mascarenes, y Lampourdos, y Souza. This
nobleman carried himself with a haughtiness

suitable to a person who bore so many names. He spoke with the most noble disdain to every one, held his head up so high, strained his voice to such a pitch, assumed so imperious an air, and stalked about with so much loftiness and pride, that every one who had the honour of conversing with him could not help longing to horsewhip his excellency. He was immoderately fond of women, and Mistress Cunégonde appeared in his eyes a paragon of beauty. The first thing he did was to ask her if she was not the captain's wife? The air with which he made this demand alarmed Candide, who did not dare to say he was married to her, because, indeed, he was not ; neither durst he say she was his sister, because she was not : and though a lye of this nature might possibly have been of some service to him in the present dilemma, yet the purity of his heart would not permit him to violate the truth. Mistress Cunégonde, replied he, intends to do me the honour to marry me, and we humbly beseech your excellency to condescend to grace the ceremony with your presence.

Don Fernando d'Ibaraa, y Figueora, y Mascarenes, y Lampourdos, y Souza, twirling his mustachio, and putting on a sarcastic sneer, ordered Captain Candide to go and review his company. The gentle Candide obeyed, and the governor was left with Mistress Cunégonde. He made her a strong declaration of love, protesting, that he was ready to give her his hand in the face of the church, or otherwise, as should appear most agreeable to a young lady of her prodigious beauty. Cunégonde desired leave to retire a quarter of an hour to consult the old woman, and determine how she should proceed.

The old woman gave her the following counsel : My dear Mistress, it is very true, you have seventy-two quarterings in your arms, but you have not a penny in your purse : it is your own fault, if you are not, in a few hours, wife to one of the greatest noblemen in South America, with an exceeding fine pair of whiskers. What business have you to pride yourself upon an unshaken constancy ? —You have been ravished by the Bulgarian soldiers, a Jew and an Inquisitor have both had you by turns. People ought to make some advantage of their misfortunes. I must confess, therefore, were I in your place, I should, without the least scruple, give my hand to the Governor, and thereby make the fortune of the brave Captain Candide. While the old woman was thus haranguing, with all the prudence that old age and experience furnish, a small bark entered the harbour, in which was an alcayde and his alguazils. Matters had fallen out as follows :

The old woman rightly guessed, that the sanctified Cordelier with the long sleeves was the person who had stolen Mistress Cunégonde's money and jewels while they and Candide were at Badajoz, in their flight from Lisbon. This same friar attempted to sell some of the diamonds to a jeweller, who presently knew them to have belonged to the Grand Inquisitor, and stopped them. The Cordelier, before he was hanged, acknowledged that he had stolen them, and described the persons, and the road they had taken. The flight of Cunégonde and Candide was no secret. They sent in pursuit of them to Cadiz ; and the vessel which had been sent, to make the greater dispatch, had now reached the port of Buenos Ayres. A report was spread, that an alcayde was going to land, and that he was in pursuit of the murderers of my Lord the Inquisitor. The prudent old woman saw in an instant what was to be done. You cannot run away, said she to Cunégonde ; but you have nothing to fear ; it was not you who killed my Lord Inquisitor : besides, as the Governor is in love with you, he will not suffer you to be ill-treated ; therefore stand your ground. Then hurrying away to Candide, Be gone, (said she) from hence this instant, or you will be burnt alive. Candide found there was no time to be lost ; but how could he part from Cunégonde, and whither could he fly for shelter ?

CHAPTER XIV

The Reception Candide and Cacambo met with among the Jesuits in Paraguay.

WHEN Candide left Cadiz he had with him a valet, such as we commonly pick up on the coasts of Spain and in the colonies. He was a true mongrel, being the fourth part only of a Spaniard, born in Tucuman. He had successively gone through the professions of a chorister, sexton, sailor, monk, pedlar, soldier, and lacquey. His name was Cacambo ; he had a great affection for his master, because his master was a mighty good kind of a man. He saddled the two Andalusian horses as quick as possible. Come, my good master, (said he,) let us follow the old woman's advice, and make all the haste we can from this place, without staying to look behind us. Candide burst into a flood of tears: O, my dear Cunégonde, must I then leave you in the very moment the Governor is going to honour us with his presence at our wedding ! Cunégonde, so far from home as you are, what will become of you ? Lord ! said Cacambo, she must do as well as she can ; women are never at a loss. Providence will take care of her, and so let us make the best of our way. But whither wilt thou carry me ?

where can we go ? what can we do without Cunégonde ? cried the disconsolate Candide. By
St. James of Compostella, (said Cacambo) ask
no more questions but resolve what to do ; you
was going to fight against the Jesuits of Paraguay ; now, let us even go and fight for them :
I know the road perfectly well ; I'll conduct you
to their kingdom ; they will be delighted with
a captain that understands the Bulgarian exercise ;
you will certainly make a prodigious fortune.
If we cannot find our account in one world, we
may in another. Besides, nothing is more agreeable than to see new objects, and enter upon new
adventures.

Then you have been in Paraguay ? said Candide. Ay, marry, have I, (replied Cacambo) :
I was a scout in the college of the Assumption,
and am as well acquainted with the new government of Los Padres, the Jesuits, as I am with the
streets of Cadiz. It is an excellent government
and a wonderful establishment, that is most
certain ! The kingdom is at present upwards
of three hundred leagues in diameter, and divided
into thirty provinces ; the fathers are there
masters of every thing, and the people have
nothing. This contrivance is the master-piece
of justice and reason. For my part, I see nothing
so holy and divine as the good fathers, who wage
war in this part of the world against the troops of
Spain and Portugal, and at the same time hear
the confessions of those very princes in Europe ;
who shoot the Spaniards in America, and send

them to heaven with the holy sacrament, at Madrid. All this pleases me exceedingly, but let us make haste ; you are going to see the happiest and most fortunate of all the inhabitants of the globe. How charmed will those fathers be to hear that a captain, who understands the Bulgarian exercise, is coming among them !

As soon as they reached the first barrier, Cacambo called to the advance-guard, and told them that a captain wanted to speak to my Lord the General. Notice was given to the main-guard, and immediately a Paraguayan officer ran to throw himself at the feet of the com-mandant to impart this news to him. Candide and Cacambo were immediately disarmed, and their two Andalusian horses were seized. The two strangers are now conducted between two files of musqueteers, the commandant was at the farther end, with a three-cornered cap on his head, his gown tucked up, a sword by his side, and an half pike in his hand ; he made a sign, and instantly four-and-twenty soldiers drew up round the new comers. A serjeant told them that they must wait, the commandant could not speak to them ; and that the reverend father provincial did not suffer any Spaniard to open his mouth but in his presence, or to stay above three hours in the province. And where is the reverend father provincial ? (said Cacambo) He is just come from mass, and is at the parade, (replied the serjeant), and you must wait three hours before you can possibly have the honour to kiss his spurs. But (said Cacambo), the captain, who, as well as myself, is perishing with hunger, is no Spaniard, but a German ; might we not be permitted to eat a morsel while we wait for his Reverence ?

The serjeant immediately went, and acquainted the commandant with what he heard. God be praised (said the reverend commandant), since he is a German, I may condescend to hear what he has to say ; let him be brought to my arbour. Immediately they conducted Candide to a beautiful pavilion, adorned with a colonade of green marble, spotted with yellow, and with an intertexture of vines, which served as a kind of cage for parrots, humming birds, fly-birds, Guinea hens, and all other curious kinds of birds. An excellent breakfast was provided in vessels of gold ; and while his Paraguayan subjects were eating coarse Indian corn out of wooden dishes in the open air, and exposed to the burning heat of the sun, the reverend father commandant retired to his cool arbour.

He was a very handsome young man, round-faced, fair, and fresh coloured, his eye-brows were finely arched, he had a piercing eye, the tips of his ears were red, his lips vermillion, and he had a bold commanding air ; but such a boldness as neither resembled that of a Spaniard nor of a Jesuit. He ordered Candide and Cacambo to have their arms restored to them, together with their two Andalusian horses. Cacambo desired the poor beasts might have some oats to eat close

by the arbour, keeping a strict eye upon them all
the while for fear of surprise.

Candide having first kissed the hem of the
commandant's robe, they sat down to table. It
seems you are a German, says the Jesuit to him
in that language? Yes, reverend father, answered Candide. As they pronounced these
words, they looked at each other with great
amazement, and with an emotion that neither
could restrain. From what part of Germany
do you come, said the Jesuit? From the dirty
province of Westphalia, answered Candide: I
was born in the castle of Thunder-ten-Tronckh.
Oh heavens! is it possible? said the commandant. What a miracle! cried Candide.
Can it be you? said the commandant. On this
they both fell backwards with amazement, then
getting up and running into each other's arms,
embraced, and let fall a shower of tears. Is it
you then, reverend father? You are the brother
of the fair Mistress Cunégonde? You that was
slain by the Bulgarians! You the Baron's son!
You a Jesuit in Paraguay! I must confess this
is a strange world we live in. O Pangloss!
Pangloss! what joy would this have given you,
if you had not been hanged.

The commandant ordered the negro slaves
and the Paraguayans, who presented them with
liquor in crystal goblets, to retire. He returned
thanks to God and St. Ignatius a thousand times;
he clasped Candide in his arms, and both their
faces were bathed in tears. You will be more

surprised, more affected, more transported, said Candide, when I tell you that Mistress Cunégonde, your sister, whose belly was supposed to have been ript open, is in perfect health. Where? In your neighbourhood, with the Governor of Buenos Ayres ; and I myself was going to fight against you. Every word they uttered, during this long conversation, introduced some fresh matter of wonder and amazement. Their souls fluttered on their tongues, listened in their ears, and sparkled in their eyes. Like true Germans, they stuck to their bottle, and continued a long time at table, waiting for the reverend father ; when the commandant spoke to his dear Candide as follows :

CHAPTER XV

How Candide killed the Brother of his dear Cunégonde.

I think I shall never forget the dreadful day when I beheld my father and mother murdered, my sister ravished by the Bulgarians. When the Bulgarians retired, my dear sister was no where to be found ; but the bodies of my father, mother, and myself, with two servant maids, and three little boys, all of whom had been murdered by the remorseless enemy, were thrown into a cart, to be buried in a chapel belonging to the Jesuits, within two leagues of our family-seat. A Jesuit sprinkled us with some holy water, which happened to be extremely salt, and a few drops of it went into my eyes : the father perceived that my eye lids stirred a little ; he put his hand upon my breast, and felt my heart beat ; upon which he gave me proper assistance, and at the end of three weeks I was perfectly recovered. You know, my dear Candide, I was very handsome ; I became still more so, and the reverend father Croust, superior of that house, took a great fancy to me ; he gave me the habit of the order, and some time afterwards I was sent to Rome. Our general wanted some recruits of young German Jesuits. The Sovereigns of Paraguay admit of as few Spanish Jesuits as possible ; they prefer those of other nations, as being more easily governed. The reverend father general looked upon me as a proper person to work in that vineyard. I set out in company with a Polander and a Tyrolese. Upon my arrival, I was honoured with a subdeaconship and a lieutenancy. Now I am colonel and priest. We shall give a warm reception to the King of Spain's troops ; I can assure you, they will be beaten first and excommunicated afterwards. Providence has sent you hither to assist us. But is it true that my dear sister Cunégonde is in the neighbourhood with the governor of Buenos

Ayres ? Candide swore that nothing could be more true ; and the tears began again to trickle down their cheeks.

The Baron was never tired of embracing Candide ; he called him his brother, his deliverer. Perhaps, said he, my dear Candide, we shall be fortunate enough to enter the town together, sword in hand, and recover my sister Cunégonde. Ah ! that is just what I wish, replied Candide, for I intended to marry her ; and I hope I shall still be able to effect it. Insolent fellow ! replied the Baron. Would you have the impudence to marry my sister, who bears seventy-two quarterings ! really I think you have an intolerable assurance, to dare so much as to mention such an audacious design to me. Candide, thunderstruck at the oddness of this speech, answered, Reverend Father, what are all the quarterings in the world, to what I have done for your sister ? I have delivered her from a Jew and an Inquisitor ; she is under many obligations to me and she is resolved to give me her hand. My Master Pangloss always told me, that mankind are by nature equal. Therefore, you may depend upon it, that I shall marry your sister. We shall see that, villain ! said the Jesuit Baron of Thunder-ten-Tronckh and struck him across the face with the flat side of his sword. Candide, in an instant, draws his rapier, and plunges it up to the hilt in the Jesuit's body ; but, in pulling it out reeking hot, he burst into tears, Good God ! cried he, I have killed my old master, my friend, my brother-in-law ; I am the mildest man in the world, and yet I have already killed three men ; and two of them were priests.

Cacambo, who standing sentry near the door of the arbour, instantly ran up. Alas ! says Candide, nothing remains, but to sell our lives as dear as possible ; they will undoubtedly look into the arbour ; we must die sword in hand. Cacambo, who had seen many of these kinds of adventures, was not at all at a loss ! he stript the baron of his Jesuit's habit, and put it upon Candide, then gave him the dead man's three-cornered cap, and made him mount on horseback. All this was done in the twinkling of an eye. Gallop, master, cried Cacambo ; every body will take you for a Jesuit going to give orders ; and we shall have passed the frontiers before they will be able to overtake us. He flew as he spoke these words, crying out aloud in Spanish, make way, make way for the reverend father colonel.

CHAPTER XVI

*What happened to our Travellers with Two Girls,
Two Monkies, and the Savages, called Oreillons.*

By the time it was known in the camp that the
German Jesuit was dead, Candide and his valet
were far enough beyond the frontiers of the
town, and in no danger of being overtaken.
The provident Cacambo had taken care to fill
his wallet with bread, chocolate, some ham, some
fruit, and a few bottles of wine. They penetrated
with their Andalusian horses into a part of the
country, where they could discover no beaten
path. At length a verdant meadow, intersected
with beautiful rivulets, opened to their view.
Cacambo advised his master to take some re-
freshment, and set him the example. How
can you desire me to feast upon ham, said Candide, when I have killed the baron's son, and am
doomed never more to see the beautiful Cunégonde ? what will it avail me to prolong a wretched
life that must be spent far from her in remorse
and despair ; and then, what will the journal of
Trevoux say ?

While he was making these mournful reflections, he still continued eating, nevertheless.
The sun was now nearly setting, when the ears

of our two wanderers were struck by some shrill notes, which seemed to be uttered by a female voice. But they could not distinguish whether they were cries of grief or joy : however, they instantly started up, full of that inquietude and apprehension, which a strange place naturally inspires. The cries proceeded from two young women who were running gently, stark naked, along the mead, while two monkies followed close at their heels biting their buttocks. Candide was touched with compassion ; he had learned to shoot at a mark while he was among the Bulgarians, and could hit a filbert in an hedge, without touching a leaf. Accordingly, he takes up his double barrel Spanish fusil, pulls the trigger and lays the two monkies dead on the spot. God be praised, my dear Cacambo, I have rescued two poor girls from a most perilous situation : if I have committed a sin in killing an Inquisitor and a Jesuit, I have made ample amends by saving the lives of these two distressed damsels. Who knows but they may be young ladies of a good family, and that this assistance I have been so happy to give them, may be of great service to us in this country.

He was about to continue, but was struck speechless at seeing the two girls affectionately embracing the dead bodies of the monkies, bathing their wounds with their tears, and rending the air with the most doleful lamentations. Really, said he to Cacambo, I should not have expected to see such a prodigious share of compassion and tenderness of heart. Master, replied the knowing valet, you have made a precious piece of work of it ; do you know that you have killed the lovers of these two ladies ! Their lovers ! Cacambo ; you are jesting ! it cannot be ! I can never believe it. Dear Sir, replied Cacambo, you are surprised at every thing ; why should you think it so strange that there should be a country where monkies insinuate themselves into the good graces of the ladies ; the fourth part of men are monkies, as I am the fourth part of a Spaniard ? Alas ! replied Candide, I remember to have heard my master Pangloss say, that such attachments as these frequently existed in former times, and that these conjunctions were productive of centaurs, fauns, and satyrs ; and that many of the ancients had seen such monsters : but I looked upon the whole as fabulous. But now you must be convinced, said Cacambo, that it is very true, and you see what use is made of those creatures who have not had such an education as a man ought to have : all I am afraid of is, that these same ladies will do us some mischief.

Upon hearing these very proper remarks of Cacambo, Candide resolved to quit the meadow and strike into a wood. There he and Cacambo supped, and after heartily cursing the grand inquisitor, the governor of Buenos Ayres, and the baron, they fell asleep on the ground. When they awoke, they were surprised to find that they could not move ; the reason was, that the Oreil-

lons who inhabit that country, and to whom the
ladies had given information of these two ſtrangers,
had bound them with cords made of the bark of
trees. They saw themselves surrounded by fifty
naked Oreillons armed with bows and arrows,
clubs, and hatchets of flint ; some were making
a fire under a large cauldron ; and others were
preparing spits, crying out one and all, A Jesuit !
a Jesuit ! we shall be revenged ; we shall have
excellent cheer ; let us eat this Jesuit ; let us
eat him up.

I told you, maſter, cried Cacambo mournfully,
that these two wenches would play us some
scurvy trick. Candide seeing the cauldron and
the spits, cried out, I suppose they are going
either to boil or roaſt us. Ah ! what would
Pangloss say if he was now to see the pure dictates
of nature in their full effect ! Every thing is
right, says he ; it may be so : but I muſt confess
it is something hard to be bereft of dear Miſtress
Cunégonde, and to be spitted or boiled by these
barbarous Oreillons. Cacambo, who never loſt
his presence of mind in diſtress, said to the disconsolate Candide, do not despair ; I underſtand a little of the jargon of these people ; I
will speak to them. Ay, pray do, said Candide,
and be sure you make them sensible of the horrid
barbarity of boiling and roaſting of human creatures, and how little of Chriſtianity there is in
such practices.

Gentlemen, said Cacambo, you think perhaps
you are going to devour a Jesuit ; if so, it is

mighty well ; nothing can be more agreeable to justice than thus to treat your enemies. Indeed, the law of nature teaches us to kill our neighbour, when it suits us, and accordingly we find this practised all over the world ; and if we do not indulge ourselves in eating him, it is because we have much better fare ; but for your parts, who have not such resources as we, it is certainly much better judged to feast upon your enemies than to throw their bodies to the fowls of the air ; and thus lose all the fruits of your victory. But surely, gentlemen, you would not chuse to eat your friends. You imagine you are going to roast a Jesuit, whereas my master is your friend, your defender, and you are going to spit the very man who has been destroying your enemies : as to myself, I am your countryman ; this gentleman is my master, and so far from being a Jesuit, give me leave to tell you, he has very lately killed one of that order, whose spoils he now wears, and which have probably occasioned your mistake. To convince you of the truth of what I say, take the habit he has now on, and carry it to the first barrier of the Jesuits kingdom, and enquire whether my master did not kill one of their officers. There will be little or no time lost by this, and you may still reserve our bodies in your power to feast on, if you should find what we have told you to be false. But, on the contrary, if you find it to be true, I am persuaded you are undoubtedly too well acquainted with the principles of the laws of society, humanity, and justice, not to use us courteously, and suffer us to depart unhurt.

This speech appeared very reasonable to the Oreillons ; they deputed two of their chiefs with all expedition to inquire into the truth of this affair, who acquitted themselves of their commission like men of sense, and soon returned with good tidings for our distressed adventurers.

Upon this, they were both loosed, and those who were going so lately to roast and boil them, now shewed them all sorts of civilities, offered them girls, gave them refreshments, and reconducted them to the confines of their country, crying before them all the way, in token of joy, he is no Jesuit, he is no Jesuit.

Candide could not help admiring the cause of his deliverance. What men ! what manners ! cried he : if I had not fortunately run Mistress Cunégonde's brother through the body, I should have infallibly been eaten alive. But, after all, pure nature is certainly right in her dictates ; since these people, instead of eating me, shewed me a thousand civilities, the moment they knew I was not a Jesuit.

CHAPTER XVII

*Candide and his Valet arrive in the Country of El
Dorado. What they saw there.*

WELL, said Cacambo to his master, when they
got to the frontiers of the Oreillons, you see, this
half of the world is no better than the other :
even take my advice, and let us return to Europe
the shortest way. But how can we get back ?
said Candide : or to what new place shall we go ?
Certainly, not to my own country ? the Bulgarians and the Abares are laying that waste with
fire and sword. If we go to Portugal, there I
shall be burnt ; and if we abide here, we are
every moment in danger of being spitted. But
how can I bring myself to quit that part of the
world which my dear Mistress Cunégonde
inhabits?

Let us turn towards Cayenne, said Cacambo ;
there we shall meet with some Frenchmen ; for
you know those gentry ramble all over the
world ; perhaps, they will be of some service to
us, and God will pity our distress, and send us
some relief.

It was not so easy to get to Cayenne. They
knew pretty well which way to travel ; but the
mountains, rivers, precipices, robbers, savages,
were dreadful obstacles in the road. Their

horses died with fatigue, and their provisions were all consumed. They subsisted a whole month upon wild fruit, till at length they came to a little river bordered with cocoa-trees ; the sight of which at once rallied their hopes, and supported their enfeebled carcases.

Cacambo, who was always giving as good advice as the old woman herself, said to Candide, You see we are almost exhausted ; we have travelled enough on foot. I spy an empty canoe near the river side ; let us fill it with cocoa-nuts, get into it, and go down with the stream ; a river always leads to some inhabited place. If we do not meet with agreeable things, we shall at least meet with something new. Agreed, replied Candide ; let us recommend ourselves to Providence.

They rowed a few leagues down the river, the banks of which were in some places covered with flowers ; in others barren ; in some parts smooth and level, and in others steep and rugged. The stream widened as they went farther on, till at length it passed under one of the frightful rocks, whose summits seemed to reach the clouds. Here our two travellers had the courage to commit themselves to the stream, which, contracting in this part, hurried them along with a dreadful noise and rapidity. At the end of four-and-twenty hours, they saw day-light again ; but their canoe was dashed to pieces against the rocks. They were obliged to creep along, from rock to rock, for the space of a league, till at last they discovered an immense horizon, bounded by a chain of inaccessible mountains. The country appeared cultivated equally for pleasure, and to produce the necessaries of life. The useful and agreeable were here equally blended. The roads were covered, or rather adorned, with carriages formed of elegant and glittering materials, in which were men and women of a surprizing beauty, drawn with great rapidity by red sheep of a very large size ; which far surpassed the finest coursers of Andalusia, Tetuan, or Mequinez.

Here is a country, however, said Candide, which exceeds even Westphalia. He and Cacambo landed near the first village they saw, at the entrance of which they perceived some children covered with tattered garments of the richest brocade, playing at quoits. Our two inhabitants of the European world amused themselves greatly with looking at them. The quoits were large, round pieces, yellow, red, and green, which cast a most glorious lustre. Our travellers picked some of them up, and they proved to be gold, emeralds, rubies, and diamonds ; the least of which would have been the greatest ornament to the superb throne of the great Mogul. Without doubt, said Cacambo, those children must be the king's sons, who are playing at quoits. As he was uttering these words, the school-master of the village appeared, who came to call them to school. There, said Candide, is the preceptor of the royal family.

The little rogues immediately quitted their diversion, leaving the quoits on the ground, with all their other play-things. Candide gathers them up, runs to the school-master, and, with a most respectful bow, presents them to him, giving him to understand by signs, that their royal highnesses had forgot their gold and precious stones. The school-master, with a smile, flung them upon the ground, then examining Candide from head to foot, with an air of admiration, he turned his back, and went on his way.

Our travellers took care, however, to gather up the gold, the rubies, and the emeralds. Where are we? for heaven's sake, cried Candide: The king's children in this country must be very properly educated, since they are taught to show such a contempt for gold and precious stones. Cacambo was as much surprised as his master. They then drew near the first house in the village, which was built after the manner of the palaces in Europe. There was a crowd of people about the door, and a still greater number in the house. The sound of the most delightful instruments of music was heard, and a most savoury smell came from the kitchen. Cacambo went up to the door, and heard those within talking in the Peruvian language, which was his mother tongue; for every one knows that Cacambo was born in a village of Tucuman, where no other language is spoken. I will be your interpreter here, said he to Candide, let us go in; this is an eating-house.

71

Immediately two waiters, and two servant-girls, dressed in cloth of gold, and their hair braided with ribbands of tissue, accost the strangers, and invite them to sit down to the ordinary. Their dinner consisted of four dishes of different soups, each garnished with two young paroquets, a large dish of bouille, that weighed two hundred weight, two roasted monkies of a delicious flavour, three hundred humming birds in one dish, and six hundred fly-birds in another ; some excellent ragouts, delicate tarts, and the whole served up in dishes of rock-crystal. Several sorts of liquors, extracted from the sugar-cane, were handed about by the servants who attended.

Most of the company were pedlars and wag-goners, all extremely polite. They asked Cacambo a few questions, with the utmost discretion and politeness ; and replied to his in a most obliging and satisfactory manner.

As soon as dinner was over, both Candide and Cacambo thought they should pay very hand-somely for their entertainment, by laying down two of those large gold pieces, which they had picked off the ground ; but the landlord and landlady burst into a fit of laughing, and held their sides for some time. At last recovering themselves, Gentlemen, said the landlord, I plainly perceive you are strangers, and such we are not accustomed to see ; pardon us, there-fore, for laughing, when you offered us the com-mon pebbles of our high-ways for payment of your reckoning. To be sure, you have none of the coin of this kingdom ; but there is no necessity of having any money at all to dine in this house. All the inns, which are established for the conveniency of those who carry on the trade of this nation, are maintained by the government. You have found but very indifferent entertainment here ; because this is only a poor village ; but in almost every other of these public houses, you will meet with a reception worthy of persons of your merit. Cacambo explained the whole of this speech of the landlord to Candide, who listened to it with the same astonishment with which his friend communicated it. What sort of a country is this, said the one to the other, that is unknown to all the world, and in which Nature has every where so different an appearance to what she has in ours ? Possibly this is that part of the globe where every thing is right, for there must certainly be some such place ; and, notwithstanding all that Dr. Pangloss could say, I often perceived that things went very ill in Westphalia.

CHAPTER XVIII

What they saw in the Country of El Dorado.

CACAMBO having the advantage of understanding the language of El Dorado, tried to satisfy his curiosity with his landlord by a thousand different questions : the honest man answered him plainly : I am very ignorant, Sir, but I am content ; however, we have in this neighbourhood an old man retired from court, who is the best informed and most communicative person in the whole kingdom. He then carried Cacambo to the old man ; Candide acted now only an under part and attended his valet. They entered a very plain house, for the door was nothing but silver, and the ceiling was only of beaten gold, but wrought in so elegant a taste as to vie with the richest. The antechamber, indeed, was only incrusted with rubies and emeralds ; but the order in which every thing was disposed made amends for this great simplicity.

The old man received the strangers on his sofa, which was stuffed with humming birds' feathers ; and ordered his servants to present them with liquors in golden goblets, after which he satisfied their curiosity in the following terms :

I am now one hundred and seventy-two years old ; and I learnt of my late father, who was equerry to the king, the amazing revolutions of Peru, to which he had been an eye-witness. This kingdom is the ancient patrimony of the Incas, who very imprudently quitted it to conquer another part of the world, and were at length conquered and destroyed themselves by the Spaniards.

Those princes of their family, who remained in their native country, acted more wisely. They made a law, with the consent of their whole nation, that none of the inhabitants of our little kingdom should ever quit it ; and to this wise ordinance we owe the preservation of our innocence and happiness. The Spaniards had some confused notion of this country, to which they gave the name of El Dorado ; and Sir Walter Raleigh, an Englishman, actually came very near it, about three hundred years ago : but the inaccessible rocks and precipices, with which our country is surrounded on all sides, has hitherto secured us from the rapacious fury of the people of Europe, who have an unaccountable fondness for the pebbles and dirt of our land, for the sake of which they would murder us all to the very last man.

The conversation lasted a considerable length of time, and turned chiefly on the form of government, their manners, their women, their public diversions, and the arts. At length, Candide, who had always had a turn for metaphysics, asked whether the people of that country had any established religion ?

The old man reddened a little at this question :
Can you doubt it ? said he ; do you take us for
wretches lost to all sense of gratitude ? Cacambo
asked in a respectful manner what was the established religion of El Dorado : The old man
blushed again, and said, can there be two religions,
then ? Ours, I apprehend, is the religion of the
whole world ; we worship God from morning
till night. Do you worship but one God ? said
Cacambo, who still acted as the interpreter of
Candide's doubts. Certainly, said the old man ;
there are not two, nor three, nor four Gods. I
must confess the people of your world ask extraordinary questions. However, Candide could
not refrain from making many more enquiries of
the old man ; he wanted to know in what manner
they prayed to God in El Dorado. We do not
pray to him at all, said the reverend sage ; we
have nothing to ask of him, he has given us all we
want, and we give him thanks incessantly. Candide had a curiosity to see some of their priests,
and desired Cacambo to ask the old man where
they were ? At which he smiling, said, My
friends, we are all of us priests, the King and
all the heads of families sing solemn hymns of
thanksgiving every morning, accompanied by five
or six thousand musicians. What ! says Cacambo,
have you no monks among you, to dispute, to
govern, to intrigue, and to burn people who are
not of the same opinion with themselves ? Do
you take us for fools ? said the old man: here
we are all of one opinion, and know not what

you mean by your monks. During the whole of this discourse, Candide was in raptures, and he said to himself, There's a prodigious difference between this place and Westphalia, and this house and the baron's castle ! If our friend Pangloss had ever seen El Dorado, never would he have maintained that the castle of Thunder-ten-Tronckh was the finest of all possible edifices : there is nothing like seeing the world, that's certain.

This long conversation being ended, the old man ordered six sheep to be harnessed, and put to the coach, and sent twelve of his servants to escort the travellers to court. Excuse me, said he, for not waiting on you in person ; my age deprives me of that honour. The king will receive you in such a manner that you will have no reason to complain ; and doubtless you will make a proper allowance for the customs of the country, if they should not happen altogether to please you.

Candide and Cacambo got into the coach, the six sheep flew, and, in less than four hours, they arrived at the king's palace, which was situated at the farther end of the capital. At the entrance was a portal two hundred and twenty feet high, and one hundred wide ; but it is impossible for words to describe the materials of which it was built. The reader, however, will readily conceive, they must have a prodigious superiority over the pebbles and sand, which we call gold and precious stones.

Candide and Cacambo were received by twenty

beautiful young virgins in-waiting, when they got out of the coach, who conducted them to the bath, and clad them in robes woven of the down of humming birds ; after which they were introduced by the great officers of the crown of both sexes to the king's apartment, between two files of musicians, each file consisting of a thousand, agreeable to the custom of the country. When they drew near to the presence chamber, Cacambo asked one of the officers in what manner they were to pay their obeisance to his majesty : whether it was the custom to fall upon their knees, or to prostrate themselves upon the ground ? whether they were to put their hands upon their heads, or behind their backs ? whether they were to lick the dust of the floor ? In short, what was the ceremony usual on such occasions ? The custom, said the great officer, is to embrace the king, and kiss him on each cheek. Candide and Cacambo accordingly threw their arms round his majesty's neck, who received them in the most gracious manner imaginable, and very politely asked them to sup with him.

In the mean time, while supper was preparing, orders were given to show them the city, where they saw public buildings, whose roofs almost touched the clouds ; the market-places decorated with a thousand columns ; fountains of spring-water, besides others of rose-water, and of liquors drawn from the sugar-cane, incessantly flowing in the great squares ; which were paved with a kind of precious stones, that emitted an odour like that of cloves and cinnamon. Candide asked to see the high court of justice, the parliament ; but was answered, that they have none in that country, being utter strangers to law-suits. He then enquired, if they had any prisons ; they replied, none. But what gave him at once the greatest surprize and pleasure was, the palace of sciences, where he saw a gallery two thousand feet long, filled with the various apparatus in mathematics and natural philosophy.

After having spent the whole afternoon in seeing only about the thousandth part of the city, they were brought back to the king's palace. Candide sat down at the table with his majesty, his valet Cacambo, and several ladies of the court. Never was entertainment more excellent and compleat in its kind, nor could any one possibly show more wit than his majesty displayed while they were at supper. Cacambo explained all the king's jests and witticisms to Candide, and what was wonderful, although they were translated, they still appeared to be excellent things. Nothing surprized Candide more than this last circumstance. They spent a whole month in this hospitable place, during which time, Candide was continually saying to Cacambo, I own, my friend, once more, that the castle where I was born is a mere nothing, in comparison of the place where we now are; but still Mistress Cunégonde is not here, and you yourself have doubtless some mistress for whom you sigh in Europe.

If we remain here, we shall only be on a level with others ; whereas, if we return to our own world with only a dozen of El Dorado sheep, loaded with the pebbles of this country, we shall be richer than all the kings in Europe ; we shall no longer need to fear the inquisitors ; and we may easily recover Mistress Cunégonde.

This speech was perfectly agreeable to Cacambo. A fondness for roving, for making a figure in their own country, and for boasting of what they had seen in their travels, was so prevalent in our two wanderers, that these two happy men resolved to be no longer happy ; and demanded permission of the king to quit the country.

You are going to do a rash and silly action, said the king ; I am sensible my kingdom is nothing very great ; but when people are tolerably at their ease in any place, I should think it would be their interest to remain there. Most assuredly I have no right to detain you or any strangers against their wills ; this is an act of tyranny to which our manners and our laws are equally repugnant : all men are by nature free ; you have therefore an undoubted liberty to depart whenever you please, but you will have many and great difficulties to encounter in passing the frontiers. It is impossible to ascend that rapid river which runs under high and vaulted rocks, and by which you were conveyed hither by a kind of miracle. The mountains by which my kingdom is hemmed in on all sides, are ten thousand feet high, and perfectly perpendicular ; they are above ten leagues over each, and the descent from them is one continued precipice. However, since you are determined to leave us, I will immediately give orders to the superintendent of my machines to cause one to be made that will convey you very safe. When they have conducted you to the back of the mountains, no body can attend you farther ; for my subjects have made a vow never to quit the kingdom, and they are too prudent to break it : Ask me whatever else you please. All we shall ask of your Majesty, said Cacambo, is only a few sheep laden with provisions, pebbles, and the clay of your country. The king smiled at the request, and said, I cannot imagine what pleasure you Europeans find in our yellow clay ; but take away as much of it as you will, and much good may it do you.

He immediately gave orders to his engineers to make a machine to hoist these two extraordinary men out of the kingdom. Three thousand good mechanics went to work, and finished it in about fifteen days ; and it did not cost more than twenty millions sterling of that country's money. Candide and Cacambo were placed on this machine, and they took with them two large red sheep, bridled and saddled, to ride upon, when they got on the other side of the mountains : twenty others to serve as sumpters for carrying provisions ; thirty laden with presents of whatever was most curious in the country ; and fifty with gold, diamonds, and other precious stones. The king, at parting with our two adventurers, embraced them with the greatest cordiality.

It was really a fine sight to behold the manner of their setting off, and the ingenious method by which they and their sheep were hoisted to the top of the mountains. The engineers took leave of them as soon as they had conveyed them to a place of safety, and Candide was wholly occupied with the thoughts of presenting his sheep to Mistress Cunégonde. Now, says he, thanks to Heaven, we have more than sufficient to pay the Governor of Buenos Ayres for Mistress Cunégonde, if she is to be had at any price. Let us make the best of our way of Cayenne, where we will take shipping, and then we may at leisure think of what kingdom we shall purchase with our riches.

CHAPTER XIX

What happened to them at Surinam, and how Candide came acquainted with Martin.

OUR travellers passed their first day's journey agreeably enough, for their spirits were kept up by knowing that they possessed more riches than were to be found in Europe, Asia, and Africa together. Candide, in the fullness of his heart,

cut the name of Mistress Cunégonde on almost
every tree he came to. The second day, two of their
sheep sunk into a morass, and were swallowed
up, with all they carried ; two more died of
fatigue ; some few days afterwards, seven or
eight perished with hunger in a desert, and others,
at different times, tumbled down precipices, or
were otherwise lost ; so that, after about an
hundred days march, they had only two sheep
left. Said Candide to Cacambo, You see, my
dear friend, how perishable the riches of this
world are ; there is nothing solid but virtue, and
the prospect of seeing Mistress Cunégonde again.
I agree with you, said Cacambo ; but we have
still two sheep left, with more treasure than ever
the king of Spain will be possessed of ; and I
espy a town at a distance, which I take to be
Surinam, a town belonging to the Dutch. We
are now at the end of our troubles, and the beginning of our pleasures.

As they approached the town, they saw a
negro slave stretched on the ground with only
one half of his habit, which was a kind of linen
frock ; for the poor man had lost his left leg,
and his right hand. My God, said Candide,
in Dutch, what dost thou here, friend, in this
deplorable condition ? I am waiting for my
master Mynheer Vanderdendur, the great merchant, answered the negro. Was it Mynheer
Vanderdendur that used you in this cruel manner ?
Yes, Sir, said the negro ; it is the custom in this
town. They give us a linen garment twice a

year, and that is all our covering. When we labour in the sugar-works, and the mill happens to snatch hold of a finger, they instantly chop off our hand ; and when we attempt to run away, they cut off a leg. Both these cases have happened to me, this is the price we pay for the sugar which you eat in Europe ; and yet when my mother sold me for ten pattacoons on the coast of Guinea, she said to me, My dear child, bless our Fetiches ; adore them for ever ; they will make the happiness of your life ; you have the honour to be a slave to our lords the whites, by which you will make the fortune of us thy parents. Alas ! I know not whether I have made their fortunes ; but I'm sure they have not made mine : dogs, monkies, and parrots, are a thousand times less wretched than me. The Dutch fetiches who converted me, tell me every Sunday, that the blacks and whites are all children of one father, whom they call Adam. As for me, I do not understand any thing of genealogies ; but if what these preachers say is true, we are all cousin Germans ; and you, at least, must allow, that it is hardly possible to treat relations in a worse manner.

O Pangloss ! cried out Candide, when you said all was for the best, such horrid doings never entered thy imagination. I give up your doctrine ; I find myself, after all, obliged to renounce thy Optimism. Optimism ! said Cacambo, what is that ? Alas ! replied Candide, it is the obstinacy of maintaining that every thing is best when it is worst : and so saying, he turned his eyes towards the poor negro, and shed a flood of tears ; and in this weeping mood he entered the town of Surinam.

The first thing our travellers did upon their arrival, was to enquire if there was any vessel in the harbour which they might send to Buenos Ayres. The person they addressed themselves to happened to be the master of a Spanish bark, who offered to agree with them on moderate terms, and appointed them a meeting at a public house. Thither Candide and his faithful Cacambo went to wait for him, taking with them their two sheep.

Candide, whose heart was always at his tongue's end, made an open recital of his adventures to the Spaniard, declaring to him at the same time his resolution of carrying off Mistress Cunégonde from the governor of Buenos Ayres. O ho ! said the ship-master, if that is the case, get whom you please to carry you to Buenos Ayres ; for my part, I wash my hands of the affair : I should be hanged and so would you. The fair Cunégonde is the Governor's favourite mistress. These words were like a clap of thunder to Candide ; he wept bitterly for a long time, and taking Cacambo aside, he says to him, I'll tell you, my dear friend, what you must do : We have each of us in our pockets to the value of five or six millions in diamonds ; you understand these matters better than I do ; you must go to Buenos Ayres and bring off Mistress Cunégonde.

If the Governor makes any difficulty, give him a million ; if he holds out give him two ; as you have not killed an Inquisitor, they will have no suspicion of you : I'll fit out another ship and go to Venice, where I will wait for you : Venice is a free country, where we shall have nothing to fear from Bulgarians, Abares, Jews, or Inquisitors. Cacambo greatly applauded this wise resolution. He was miserable at the thoughts of parting with so good a master, who was now his bosom friend ; but the pleasure of being able to do him a service soon got the better of his sorrow. They embraced each other with a flood of tears. Candide charged him not to forget the old woman. Cacambo set out the same day. This Cacambo was a thorough honest man.

Candide continued some days longer at Surinam, waiting for any captain to carry him and his two remaining sheep to Italy. He hired domestics, and purchased many things necessary for a long voyage ; at length, Mynheer Vanderdendur, skipper of a large Dutch vessel, came and offered his service. What will you have, said Candide, to carry me, my servants, my baggage, and these two sheep you see here, directly to Venice ? The skipper asked ten thousand piastres ; and Candide agreed to his demand without hesitation.

Ho, ho ! said the cunning Vanderdendur to himself, this stranger must be very rich ; he agrees to give me ten thousand piastres without hesitation. Returning a little while after, he tells Candide, that upon second thoughts he could not undertake the voyage for less than twenty thousand. Very well, you shall have them, said Candide.

Zounds ! said the skipper to himself, this man agrees to pay twenty thousand piastres with as much ease as ten. Accordingly he goes back again, and tells him roundly that he will not carry him to Venice for less than thirty thousand piastres. Then you shall have thirty thousand, said Candide.

Odso! said the Dutch captain once more to himself, thirty thousand piastres is nothing to this man. Those sheep must certainly be laden with an immense treasure. I'll ask no more at present ; but make him pay down the thirty thousand piastres, and then we may see what is to be done farther. Candide sold two small diamonds, the least of which was worth more than all the skipper asked. He paid him beforehand, the two sheep were put on board, and Candide followed in a small boat to join the vessel in the road. The skipper takes his opportunity, hoists his sails, and puts out to sea with a favourable wind. Candide, distracted and amazed, soon lost sight of the ship. Alas ! said he, this is a trick like those in our old world ! He returns back to the shore overwhelmed with grief ; and, indeed he had reason, for he had lost the treasures of twenty kingdoms.

Immediately upon his landing, he applied to

the Dutch magistrate : being in great agitation,
he thunders at the door, which being opened, he
goes in, tells his case, and talks a little louder than
was necessary. The magistrate began with
fining him ten thousand piastres for the noise
he had made, and then listened very patiently
to what he had to say, promised to examine into
the affair at the skipper's return, and ordered
him to pay ten thousand piastres more for the
fees of the hearing. This treatment made
Candide almost mad : it is true he had suffered
misfortunes a thousand times more grievous ;
but the unfeeling coolness of the judge, and the
villainy of the skipper, raised his choler and
threw him into a deep melancholy. The villainy
of mankind presented itself to his mind in all its
deformity, and his mind was a prey to the most
gloomy ideas. After some time, hearing that
the captain of a French ship was ready to set sail
for Bourdeaux, as he had no more sheep loaded
with diamonds to put on board, he hired the cabin
at the common price ; and then gave publick
notice in the town that he would pay the passage
and board of any honest man who would give him
his company during the voyage ; besides making
him a present of ten thousand piastres, provided
that such person was the most dissatisfied with
his condition, and the most unfortunate man in
the whole province.

Upon this, there appeared such a crowd of
candidates, that a large fleet could not have con-
tained them. Candide, willing to chuse from

among those who appeared most likely to answer
his intention, selected twenty, who seemed to him
the most sociable, and who all pretended to merit
the preference. He invited them to his inn,
and promised to treat them with a supper, on
condition that every man should bind himself
by an oath to relate his own history ; declaring,
at the same time, that he would make choice of
that person who should appear to him the most
deserving of compassion, and the most justly
dissatisfied with his condition of life ; and that
he would make a present to the rest.

This extraordinary assembly continued sitting
till four in the morning. Candide, while he was
listening to their adventures, called to mind what
the old woman had said to him in their voyage to
Buenos Ayres, and the wager she had laid, that
there was not a person on board the ship but had
met with some great misfortune. Every story
he heard put him in mind of Pangloss. My old
master, said he, would be hard put to it to support
his favourite system. Would he were here !
Certainly if every thing is for the best, it is in El
Dorado, and not in any other part of the world.
At length he determined in favour of a poor
scholar, who had been a hackney writer ten
years for the booksellers at Amsterdam ; being
of opinion that no employment could be more
disgusting or intolerable.

This scholar, who was in fact a very honest
man, had been robbed by his wife, beat by his
son, and forsaken by his daughter, who contrived

to persuade a Portuguese to run away with her. He had been likewise deprived of a small employment on which he subsisted, and he was persecuted by the clergy of Surinam, who took him for a Socinian. It must be acknowledged, that the other competitors were, at least, as wretched as he ; but Candide was in hopes that the company of a man of letters would relieve the tediousness of the voyage. All the other candidates complained that Candide had done them great injustice ; but he stopped their mouths by a present of an hundred piastres to each.

CHAPTER XX

What befel Candide and Martin on their Passage.

THE old scholar, whom Candide had preferred to the other miserable claimants, was named Martin, and took shipping with Candide for Bourdeaux. They both had seen and suffered a great deal ; and had the ship been to sail from Surinam to Japan, round the Cape of Good Hope, they could have found sufficient subject for conversation during the whole voyage, in declaiming upon moral and natural evil.

Candide, however, had one great advantage

over Martin, which was, that he ſtill kept up the
hope of seeing Miſtress Cunégonde once more ;
whereas the poor philosopher had nothing at all
left to hope for : besides, Candide had money
and jewels, and, notwithſtanding he had loſt an
hundred large red sheep, laden with the greateſt
treasure on the earth, and though the Dutch
skipper's knavery ſtill vexed him at the heart,
yet when he considered what he had ſtill left in
his pocket, and repeated the name of Cunégonde,
especially after a good dinner, he inclined to
Pangloss's doctrine.

Pray now, said he, Mr. Martin, what is your
opinion of the whole of this syſtem ? what
notion have you of moral and natural evil ? Sir,
replied Martin, our prieſt accused me of being a
Socinian ; but the real truth is, I am a Manichæan. Surely you are jeſting, said Candide ;
there are no Manichæans exiſting at present in
the world. Yes, I am one, said Martin ; but I
cannot help it ; I cannot for the life of me think
otherwise. The devil muſt be in you then, said
Candide. Perhaps he is, said Martin, for he
busies himself so much in the affairs of the world,
that it is very probable he may be in me, as well
as every where else ; but I muſt confess, when
I caſt my eye on this globe, or rather globule, I
cannot help thinking, that God has given it up
to the management of some malignant being. I
always except El Dorado. I scarce ever know a
city that did not wish the deſtruction of its neighbouring city ; nor a family that did not desire

H   91

to exterminate some other family. The poor, in all parts of the world, bear an inveterate hatred to the rich, even while they submit to, and fawn upon them ; and the rich treat the poor like sheep, whose wool and flesh they barter for money : a million of regimental assassins traverse Europe from one end to the other, to get their bread by authorized plunder and murder, because it is the most gentleman-like profession. Even in those cities which seem to enjoy the blessings of peace, and where the arts flourish, the inhabitants are devoured with envy, care, and inquietudes, which are greater plagues than any experienced in a town besieged. Private chagrins are still more dreadful than public calamities. In a word, said Martin, I have seen and suffered so much, that I am a Manichæan.

And yet there is some good in the world, replied Candide. May be so, said Martin, but it has never fallen within my notice.

While they were deeply engaged in this dispute, they heard the report of a cannon, which redoubled every moment. Each takes out his glass, and they discover two ships hotly engaged at the distance of about three miles. The wind brought them both so near the French ship, that those on board her had the pleasure of seeing the fight with great ease. At last one of the ships gave the other a shot between wind and water, which sunk her in an instant. Candide and Martin then plainly perceived an hundred men on the deck of the vessel which was sinking, who, with hands uplifted to heaven, sent forth piercing cries, and were in a moment swallowed up by the waves.

Well, said Martin, you now see in what manner mankind treat each other. It is certain, said Candide, that there is something diabolical in this business. As he was speaking thus, he spied something of a shining red hue, which swam close to the vessel. The boat was hoisted out to see what it might be, when it proved to be one of his sheep. Candide felt more joy at the recovery of this one animal, than he did grief when he lost the other hundred, though laden with the large diamonds of El Dorado.

The French captain quickly perceived that the ship which had sunk the other was a Spaniard, that the other was a Dutch pirate, and the very same captain who had robbed Candide. The immense riches which this villain had amassed were buried with him in the deep, and only this one sheep saved out of the whole. You see, said Candide to Martin, that crimes are sometimes punished ; this villain, the Dutch skipper, has met with the fate he deserved. Very true, said Martin ; but why should the passengers be doomed also to destruction ? God has punished the rogue, but the devil has drowned the rest.

The French and Spanish ships continued their cruise, and Candide and Martin continued their conversation. They disputed fourteen days successively, at the end of which, they were just as far advanced as the first moment they began.

However, they had the satisfaction of conversing, of communicating their ideas, and of mutually comforting each other. Candide embraced his sheep with transport : Since I have found thee again so unexpectedly, said he, I may possibly find Mistress Cunégonde again.

CHAPTER XXI

Candide and Martin, while thus reasoning with each other, draw near the Coast of France.

At length they came within sight of the coast of France, when Candide said to Martin, Pray, Mr. Martin, was you ever in France ? Yes, Sir, said Martin, I have passed through several provinces of that kingdom. In some, one half of the people are fools ; in some, they are too artful ; in others again, they are, in general, very simple, and very stupid ; while in others, they affect to be witty, and in all, their ruling passion is love, the next is slander, and the last is to talk nonsense. But pray, Mr. Martin, was you ever in Paris ? Yes, Sir, I have been in that city, and there you find all the several species just described ; it is a chaos, a croud, where every one seeks for pleasure, without being able to find it ; at least, as far as

94

I have observed of their conduct ; I stayed there
but a short time. I scarce had set my foot in the
place, before I was robbed of all I had in the
world by pick-pockets and sharpers, at the fair
of St. Germain. I was taken up myself for a
robber, and confined in prison a whole week ;
after which, I hired myself as corrector to a
press, in order to get a little money towards de-
fraying my expences back to Holland on foot.
I knew the whole mob of scribblers, malcontents,
and fanatics. It is said, the people of that city
are very polite ; perhaps they are so.

I cannot say, said Candide, that I have any
great curiosity to see France ; you may easily
conceive, my friend, that, after spending a month
at El Dorado, I can desire to behold nothing upon
earth but Mistress Cunégonde ; I am going to
wait for her at Venice ; I intend to pass through
France, on my way to Italy ; will you not go with
me ? With all my heart, said Martin ; they say,
that none but noble Venetians pass their time
agreeably at Venice ; but that, nevertheless,
strangers are well received there, when they have
plenty of money ; now I have none, but you have,
therefore I will attend you whither you please.
Now we are upon this subject, said Candide, Do
you think that the earth was originally sea, as we
read in that great book which belongs to the
captain of the ship ? I believe nothing of it,
replied Martin, any more than I do of the many
other strange things which have been handed
down to us for some time past. But then, to

what end, said Candide, was the world formed ?
To turn our brains, said Martin. Are you not
surprised, continued Candide, at the love which
the two girls in the country of the Oreillons
had for those two monkies ?—You know I have
told you the story. Surprised ! replied Martin,
not in the least ; I see nothing strange in this
passion. I have seen so many extraordinary
things, that there is nothing extraordinary to me
now. Do you think, said Candide, that mankind always massacred each other as they do
now ? Were they always guilty of lies, fraud,
treachery, ingratitude, inconstancy, envy, ambition, and cruelty ? Were they always thieves,
fools, cowards, gluttons, drunkards, misers,
calumniators, debauchees, fanatics, and hypo-
crites ? Do you believe, said Martin, that
hawks have always been accustomed to eat
pigeons when they came in their way ? Doubtless, said Candide. Well then, replied Martin,
if hawks have always had the same nature, why
should you pretend that mankind change theirs ?
Oh ! said Candide, there is a great deal of
difference, for free will—but in the midst of
the argument, they arrive at Bourdeaux.

CHAPTER XXII

What happened to Candide and Martin in France.

CANDIDE ſtopt not a moment longer at Bourdeaux,
than was necessary to dispose of a few of the pebbles he had brought from El Dorado, and to
provide himself with a good chaise that would
carry two persons, for he could no longer ſtir
a ſtep without his philosopher Martin. The
only thing that gave him concern, was the being
obliged to leave his sheep behind him, which he
left with the learned members of the academy of
sciences at Bourdeaux, who proposed, as a prize-
subjeƈt for the year, to inveſtigate the cause why
the wool of this sheep was red ; and the prize
was adjudged to a northern sage, who demon-
ſtrated by A plus B, minus C, divided by Z, that
the sheep muſt necessarily be red, and die of the
rot.

In the mean time, all the travellers whom
Candide met with in the inns, or on the road, told
him to a man that they were going to Paris.
This general eagerness seemed very extraordinary,
and gave him a great desire to see this capital,
and it was not much out of the way to Venice.

He entered the city by the suburbs of St.
Marceau, and thought himself in one of the
vileſt hamlets in all Weſtphalia.

Candide had not been long at his inn, before he was seized with a slight disorder, owing to the fatigue he had undergone. As he wore a diamond of an enormous size on his finger, and had, among the rest of his equipage, a strong box that seemed very weighty, he soon found himself beset by two physicians, whom he had not sent for, a number of intimate friends whom he had never seen, and who would not quit his bed-side, and two female devotees, who were very careful in cooking broths for him.

I remember, said Martin to him, that the first time I came to Paris, I was likewise taken ill : But I was very poor, and, accordingly, I had neither friends, nurses, nor physicians, and yet I recovered.

However, by dint of purging and bleeding, Candide's disorder became very serious. The priest of the parish came with all imaginable politeness to desire a note of him, payable to the bearer in the other world. Candide refused to comply with his request ; but the two devotees assured him that it was a new fashion. Candide replied, that he was not one that followed the fashion. Martin was for throwing the priest out of the window. The priest swore Candide should not have christian burial ; Martin swore in his turn, that he would bury the priest alive, if he continued to plague them any longer. The dispute grew warm ; Martin took him by the shoulders, and turned him out of the room, which gave great scandal, and occasioned an action at law.

Candide recovered ; and, till he was in a condition to go abroad, had a great deal of very good company to pass the evenings with him in his chamber. They played deep. Candide was surprised to find he could never win a trick : but Martin was not at all surprised at the matter.

Among those who did him the honours of the place, was a little spruce Abbé of Perigord, one of those insinuating, busy, fawning, impudent, necessary fellows, that lay wait for strangers at their arrival, tell them all the scandal of the town, and offer to minister to their pleasures at various prices. This man conducted Candide upon his recovery and Martin to the playhouse ; they were acting a new tragedy. Candide was placed near a cluster of wits : This, however, did not prevent his shedding tears at some parts of the piece which were most affecting, and best acted. One of these critics said to him between the acts, You are greatly to blame to shed tears ; that actress plays horribly, and the man that plays with her still worse ; and the piece itself is still more execrable than the representation. The author does not understand a word of Arabic, and yet he has laid his scene in Arabia ; and what is more, he is a fellow who does not believe in innate ideas. To-morrow I will bring you a score of pamphlets that have been wrote against him. Pray, Sir, said Candide to the Abbé, how many theatrical pieces have you in France ? Five or six thousand, replied the other. Indeed ! that is a great number, said Candide : but how

many good ones may there be ? About fifteen
or sixteen. Oh ! that is a great number of
good ones, said Martin.

Candide was greatly taken with an actress who
performed the part of Queen Elizabeth in a dull
kind of tragedy that is played sometimes. That
actress, said he to Martin, pleases me greatly ;
she has some sort of resemblance to Mistress
Cunégonde. I should be very glad to pay my
respects to her. The Abbé of Perigord offered
his service to introduce him to her at her own
house. Candide, who was brought up in Germany, desired to know what might be the cere-
monial used on those occasions, and how a Queen
of England was treated in France. There is a
necessary distinction to be observed in these
matters, said the Abbé. In a country-town we
take them to a tavern ; here, in Paris, they are
treated with great respect during their lifetime,
provided they are handsome, and when they die
we throw their bodies upon a dunghill. How,
said Candide, throw a queen's body upon a dunghill ! The gentleman is quite right, said Martin;
he tells you nothing but the truth. I happened
to be at Paris when Miss Monimia made her
exit, as one may say, out of this world into another.
She was refused what they call here the right of
sepulture ; that is to say, she was denied the
privilege of rotting in a church-yard, by the side
of all the beggars in the parish. They buried her
at the corner of Burgundy-street, which must
certainly have shocked her extremely, as she had

very exalted notions of things. This is acting very unpolitely, said Candide. Lord ! said Martin, what can be said to it ? it is the way of these people. Figure to yourself all the contradictions, all the inconsistencies possible, and you may meet with them in the government, the courts of justice, the churches, and the public spectacles of this odd nation. Is it true, said Candide, that the people of Paris are always laughing ? Yes, replied the Abbé, but it is with anger in their hearts ; they express all their complaints by loud bursts of laughter, and commit the most detestable crimes with a smile on their faces.

Who was that great overgrown beast, said Candide, who spoke so ill to me of the piece with which I was so much affected, and of the players who gave me so much pleasure ? A very good for nothing sort of a man, I assure you, answered the Abbé, one who gets his livelihood by abusing every new book and play that is written or performed ; he abominates to see any one meet with success, like eunuchs, who detest every one that possesses those powers they are deprived of ; he is one of those vipers in literature who nourish themselves with their own venom ; a pamphlet-monger. A pamphlet-monger ! said Candide, what is that ? Why a pamphlet-monger, replied the Abbé, is a writer of pamphlets.

Candide, Martin, and the Abbé of Perigord argued thus on the stair-case, while they stood to see the people go out of the playhouse. Though

I am very earnest to see Mistress Cunégonde again, said Candide, yet I have a great inclination to sup with M. Clairon, for I am really much taken with her.

The Abbé was a person of sufficient consequence to show his face at this lady's house, which was frequented by none but the best company. She is engaged this evening, said he, but I will do myself the honour to introduce you to a lady of quality of my acquaintance, at whose house you will see as much of the manners of Paris as if you had lived here for forty years.

Candide, who was naturally curious, suffered himself to be conducted to this lady's house, which was in the suburbs of St. Honoré. The company were engaged at basset ; twelve melancholy punters held each in his hand a small pack of cards, the corners of which, doubled down, were so many registers of their ill fortune. A profound silence reigned through the assembly, a pallid dread had taken possession of the countenances of the punters, and restless inquietude stretched every muscle of the face of him who kept the bank ; and the lady of the house, who was seated next to him, observed with lynx's eyes every *parole* and *sept le va* as they were going, as likewise those who tallied, and made them undouble their cards with a severe exactness, though mixed with a politeness, which she thought necessary, not to frighten away her customers. This lady assumed the title of Marchioness of Parolignac. Her daughter, a

girl of about fifteen years of age, was one of the
punters, and took care to give her mamma an
item, by signs, when any one of them attempted
to repair the rigour of their ill fortune by a little
innocent deception. The company were thus
occupied, when Candide, Martin, and the Abbé
made their entrance : not a creature rose to
salute them, or indeed took the leaſt notice of
them, being wholly intent upon the business in
hand. Ah ! said Candide, my Lady Baroness
of Thunder-ten-Tronckh would have behaved
more civilly.

However, the Abbé whispered the Marchioness
in the ear, who, half raising herself from her seat,
honoured Candide with a gracious smile, and
gave Martin a nod of her head, with an air of
inexpressible dignity. She then ordered a seat
for Candide, and desired him to make one at their
party of play : he did so, and, in a few deals loſt
near a thousand pieces ; after which they supped
very elegantly, and every one was surprised at
seeing Candide lose so much money, without
appearing to be the leaſt diſturbed at it. The
servants in waiting said to each other, This is
certainly some English lord.

The supper was like moſt others of this kind
at Paris. At firſt every one was silent ; then
followed a few confused murmurs, and afterwards several insipid jokes passed and repassed,
with false reports, false reasonings, a little politics,
and a great deal of scandal. The conversation
then turned upon the new produćtions in litera-

ture. Pray, said the Abbé, good folks, have you
seen the romance written by the Sieur Gauchat,
doctor of divinity ? Yes, answered one of the
company, but I had not patience to go through
it. The town is pestered with a swarm of impertinent productions, but this, of Dr. Gauchat's,
outdoes them all. In short, I was so cursedly
tired of reading this vile stuff, that I even resolved
to come here, and make a party at basset.——
But what say you to the Archdeacon T————'s
Miscellaneous Collection ? said the Abbé. Oh
my God ! cried the Marchioness of Parolignac,
never mention the tedious creature ! only think
what pains he is at to tell one things that all the
world knows, and how he labours an argument
that is hardly worth the slightest consideration !
how absurdly he makes use of other people's
wit ! how miserably he mangles what he has
pilfered from them ! The man makes me quite
sick ! A few pages of the good Archdeacon
are enough in conscience to satisfy any one.

There was at the table a person of learning and
taste, who supported what the Marchioness had
advanced.—They next began to talk of tragedies.
The lady desired to know how it came about that
so many tragedies still continued to be acted,
though they would not bear reading ? The man
of taste explained very clearly, how a piece may be
in some manner interesting, without having a
grain of merit. He shewed, in a few words,
that it is not sufficient to throw together a few
incidents that are to be met with in every romance,

104

and that dazzle the spectator ; but that the thoughts should be new, without being far-fetched ; frequently sublime, but always natural : the author should have a thorough knowledge of the human heart, and make it speak properly ; he should be a complete poet, without showing an affectation of it in any of the characters of his piece ; he should be a perfect master of his language, speak it with all its purity, and with the utmost harmony, and yet so as not to make the sense a slave to the rhyme. Whoever, added he, neglects any one of these rules, though he may write two or three tragedies with tolerable success, will never be reckoned in the number of good authors. There are very few good tragedies ; some are idylliums, in well-written and har-monious dialogue ; and others a chain of political reasonings that set one asleep, or else pompous and high-flown amplifications, that disgust rather than please. Others again are the ravings of a madman, in an uncouth style, unmeaning flights, or long apostrophes to the deities, for want of knowing how to address mankind : in a word, a collection of false maxims and dull common-place.

Candide listened to this discourse with great attention, and conceived an high opinion of the person who delivered it ; and as the Marchioness had taken care to place him near her side, he took the liberty to whisper her softly in the ear, and ask who this person was that spoke so well ? He is a man of letters, replied her ladyship, who never plays, and whom the Abbé brings with him to my house sometimes to spend an evening. He is a great judge of writing, especially in tragedy : he has composed one himself, which was damned, and has written a book that was never seen out of his bookseller's shop, excepting only one copy, which he sent with a dedication, to which he had prefixed my name. Oh ! the great man, cried Candide, he is a second Pangloss.

Then turning towards him, Sir, said he, you are doubtless of opinion that every thing is for the beſt in the physical and moral world, and that nothing could be otherwise than it is ? I, Sir ! replied the man of letters, I think no such thing, I assure you ; I find that all in this world is set the wrong end uppermoſt. No one knows what is his rank, his office, nor what he does, nor what he should do ; and that except our evenings, which we generally pass tolerably merrily, the reſt of our time is spent in idle disputes and quarrels, Janseniſts againſt Moliniſts, the parliament againſt the church, and one armed body of men againſt another ; courtier againſt courtier, husband againſt wife, and relations againſt relations. In short, this world is nothing but one continued scene of civil war.

Yes, said Candide, and I have seen worse than all that ; and yet a learned man, who had the misfortune to be hanged, taught me that every thing was marvellously well, and that these evils you are speaking of were only so many shades in the beautiful picture. Your hempen sage, said

Martin, laughed at you ; these shades, as you call them, are most horrible blemishes. The men make these blemishes, rejoined Candide, and they cannot do otherwise. Then it is not their fault, added Martin. The greatest part of the gamesters, who did not understand a syllable of this discourse, amused themselves with drinking, while Martin reasoned with the learned gentleman ; and Candide entertained the lady of the house with a part of his adventures.

After supper the Marchioness conducted Candide into her dressing room, and made him sit down under a canopy. Well, said she, are you still so violently fond of Mistress Cunégonde of Thunder-ten-Tronckh? Yes, Madam, replied Candide. The Marchioness says to him, with a tender smile, You answer me like a young man born in Westphalia ; a Frenchman would have said,—It is true, Madam, I had a great passion for Mistress Cunégonde ; but since I have seen you, I fear I can no longer love her as I did. Alas ! Madam, replied Candide, I will make you what answer you please. You fell in love with her, I find, in stooping to pick up her handkerchief which she had dropped ; you shall pick up my garter. With all my heart, madam, said Candide, and he picked it up. But you must tie it on again, said the lady. Candide tied it on again. Lookye, young man, said the Marchioness, you are a stranger, I make some of my lovers here in Paris languish for me a whole fortnight ; but I surrender to you the first night, because I am willing to do the honours of my country to a young Westphalian. The fair one having cast her eye on two very large diamonds that were upon the young stranger's finger, praised them in so earnest a manner, that they were in an instant transferred from his finger to hers.

As Candide was going home with the Abbé, he felt some qualms of conscience, for having been guilty of infidelity to Mistress Cunégonde. The Abbé took part with him in his uneasiness ; he had but an inconsiderable share in the thousand pieces Candide had lost at play, and the two diamonds, which had been in a manner extorted from him, and therefore very prudently designed to make the most he could of his new acquaintance, which chance had thrown in his way. He talked much of Mistress Cunégonde ; and Candide assured him, that he would heartily ask pardon of that fair one for his infidelity to her, when he saw her at Venice.

The Abbé redoubled his civilities, and seemed to interest himself warmly in every thing that Candide said, did, or seemed inclined to do.

And so, Sir, you have an engagement at Venice ? Yes, Monsieur l'Abbé, answered Candide, I must absolutely wait upon Mistress Cunégonde : and then the pleasure he took in talking about the object he loved, led him insensibly to relate, according to custom, part of his adventures with that illustrious Westphalian beauty.

I fancy, said the insinuating Abbé, Mistress Cunégonde has a great deal of wit, and writes most charming letters. I never received any from her, said Candide ; for you are to consider, that having been driven out of the castle upon her account, I could not write to her, and soon after my departure I heard she was dead ; when by mere chance I found her again. I lost her again after this, and now I have sent a messenger to her, near two thousand leagues from hence, and wait here for his return with an answer from her.

The artful Abbé listened attentively to all this, and seemed to be very thoughtful. He soon took his leave of the two adventurers, after having embraced them with the greatest cordiality. The next morning, almost as soon as his eyes were open, Candide received the following billet :

" My dearest lover,—I have been confined by illness in this city these eight days. I have heard of your arrival, and should fly to your arms, were I able to stir. I was informed of your being on the way hither to Bourdeaux, where I left the faithful Cacambo, and the old woman, who will soon follow me. The Governor of Buenos Ayres has taken every thing from me but your heart, which I still retain. Come to me immediately on the receipt of this. Your presence will either give me new life, or kill me with the pleasure."

At the receipt of this charming, this unexpected letter, Candide was in raptures, though, on the other hand, the indisposition of his beloved Mistress Cunégonde overwhelmed him with grief. Divided between these two passions, he takes his gold and his diamonds, and procured a person to conduct him and Martin to the house where Mistress Cunégonde lodged. Upon entering the room, he trembled from head to foot, his heart beat, his tongue faultered, he attempted to undraw the curtain, and called for a light to the bedside. Lord, Sir, cried a maid servant, what are you going to do, Mistress cannot bear the least light : and immediately, she pulls the curtain close again. My dear Cunégonde ! cried Candide, bursting into tears, how do you do ? If you cannot bear the light, speak to me at least. Alas ! she cannot speak, said the maid. The sick lady then puts a plump hand out of the bed, and Candide first bathes it with his tears, then fills it with diamonds, leaving a purse of gold upon the chair by the bedside.

In the midst of his transports comes an officer into the room, followed by the Abbé, and a file of musqueteers. There, said he, are the two suspected foreigners ; at the same time, he orders his men to secure them and carry them to prison. Travellers are not treated in this manner in the country of El Dorado, said Candide. I am more a Manichæan now than ever, said Martin. But pray, good Sir, where are you going to carry us ? said Candide. To a dungeon, my dear Sir, replied the officer.

When Martin became a little cool, so as to

form some judgment of what had passed, he plainly perceived, that the person who had acted the part of Mistress Cunégonde was a cheat ; that the Abbé of Perigord was a sharper, who had imposed upon the honest simplicity of Candide, and that the officer was a knave, whom they might easily get rid of.

Candide, having consulted his friend Martin, and burning with impatience to see the real Mistress Cunégonde, rather than wait the delays of a court of justice, proposes to the officer to make him a present of three small diamonds, each of them worth three thousand pistoles. Ah, Sir ! said the man with the ivory tipstaff, had you committed ever so many crimes, I must certainly think you the honestest man living. Three diamonds, worth three thousand pistoles ! Why, my dear Sir, so far from carrying you to jail, I would lose my life to serve you. There are orders for stopping all strangers ; but leave it to me ; I have a brother at Dieppe, in Normandy ; I myself will conduct you thither, and if you have a diamond left to give him, he will take as much care of you as I myself should.

But why, said Candide, do they stop all strangers ? The Abbé of Perigord made answer, That it was because a poor devil of the country of Atrebata heard some body tell foolish stories, and this induced him to commit a parricide ; not such a one as that in the month of May, 1610, but such as that in the month of December, in the year 1594, and such as many that have been perpetrated in other months and years, by other poor devils, who had heard foolish stories.

The officer then explained to them what the Abbé meant. Horrid monsters, exclaimed Candide, is it possible that such scenes should pass among a people who are perpetually singing and dancing ! Is there no flying this abominable country immediately, this execrable kingdom, where monkies provoke tigers ? I have seen bears in my country, but men I have beheld no where but in El Dorado. For God's sake, Sir, said he to the officer, conduct me to Venice, where I am to wait for Mistress Cunégonde. Really, Sir, replied the officer, I cannot possibly wait on you farther than Normandy. So saying, he ordered Candide's irons to be struck off ; acknowledged himself mistaken, and sent his followers about their business, after which he conducted Candide and Martin to Dieppe, and left them to the care of his brother. There happened just then to be a small Dutch ship in the road. The Norman, with the help of three diamonds, became the most obliging, serviceable being that ever breathed, and embarked Candide and his attendants safe on board the vessel that was just ready to sail for Portsmouth in England. This was not the strait road to Venice indeed ; but Candide thought himself delivered out of hell, and thought he should quickly find an opportunity of resuming his voyage to Venice.

CHAPTER XXIII

*Candide and Martin touch upon the English Coast;
what they see there.*

As soon as they were safe on board the Dutch
vessel, Candide could not help exclaiming, Ah
Pangloss! Pangloss! ah Martin! Martin!
ah my dear Mistress Cunégonde! what sort of a
world is this? Why, something very foolish,
and very abominable, said Martin. You know
something of England, said Candide; are they
as great fools in that country as in France? Yes;
but their folly is of a different cast, answered
Martin. You know that these two nations are
at war, about a few acres of snow in the neighbourhood of Canada, and that they have spent
more money already in the contest than all
Canada is worth. To say exactly whether there
are a greater number of people fit for Bedlam
in the one country than the other, exceeds the
limits of my imperfect capacity; I know, in
general, that the people we are going to visit,
are of a very serious and gloomy disposition.

As they were chatting thus together, they
arrived at Portsmouth. The shore, on each side
the harbour, was lined with a multitude of people,
whose eyes were stedfastly fixed on a corpulent
man, who was kneeling down on the deck of one

113

of the men of war, with something tied before his eyes. Opposite to this personage stood four soldiers, each of whom discharged three bullets into his head, with all the composure imaginable ; and when it was done, the whole company went away perfectly well satisfied. What is all this for ? said Candide ; and what cursed devil is it which thus infests and spreads his influence over the world ? He then asked, who that fat man was who had been sent out of the world with so much ceremony ? He received for answer, that it was an Admiral. And, pray, why do you put your Admiral to death ? Because he did not kill men enough himself. You must know, he had an engagement with a French Admiral, and it has been proved against him, that he was not near enough to his antagonist. But surely then replied Candide, the French Admiral must have been as far from him. There is no doubt of that, said the other ; but in this country it is found requisite, now and then, to put one Admiral to death, in order to encourage the others to fight.

Candide was so shocked at what he saw and heard, that he would not set foot on shore, but agreed with the Dutch skipper (were he even to rob him like the Captain of Surinam) to carry him directly to Venice.

In two days the Dutchman was ready. They sailed along the coast of France, and passed within sight of Lisbon, at which Candide trembled. From thence they entered the straits, and the

Mediterranean, and at length arrived at Venice. God be praised, said Candide, embracing Martin, this is the place where I am to behold my beloved Cunégonde once again. I can depend upon Cacambo, like another self. All is well, very well; every thing goes on as well as possible.

CHAPTER XXIV

Of Pacquette and Friar Giroflée.

As soon as they set foot on shore at Venice, Candide went in search of Cacambo at every inn and coffeehouse, and among all the ladies of pleasure; but could not find him. He sent every day to enquire what ships were come in, still no news of Cacambo! Said he to Martin, What! have I had time to sail from Surinam to Bourdeaux; to travel from thence to Paris, to Dieppe, to Portsmouth; to sail along the coast of Portugal and Spain, and up the Mediterranean, to spend some months at Venice; and, yet my lovely Cunégonde is not arrived! Instead of her, I only met with an infamous jade at Paris, and a rascally Abbé of Perigord. Cunégonde is certainly dead, and I have nothing to do but to follow her. Alas! how much better would it

115

have been for me to have remained in the paradise of El Dorado, than to have returned to this cursed Europe ! How just are your sentiments, my dear Martin ; you are certainly in the right ; all is misery and deceit in this wicked world.

He fell into a deep melancholy, and neither went to the opera then in fashion, nor partook of any of the diversions of the Carnival ; nor could the fairest face attract his notice. Martin said to him, Upon my word, I think you are very simple to imagine that a rascally valet, with five or six millions in his pocket, would go in search of your mistress to the further end of the world, and bring her to Venice to meet you. If he finds her, he will keep her for himself ; if he does not, he will take another. Let me advise you to think no more of your valet Cacambo, or your Mistress Cunégonde. Martin was no better than one of Job's comforters. Candide's melancholy increased, and Martin never left proving to him, that there is very little virtue and happiness in this world ; except, perhaps, in El Dorado, where it is hardly possible for any one to go.

While they were canvassing this important subject, and still expecting Mistress Cunégonde, Candide perceived a young Theatin Friar in St. Mark's Place, with a girl under his arm. The Theatin looked fresh coloured, plump, and vigorous ; his eyes sparkled ; his air and gait were bold and spirited. The girl was very pretty, and was singing a song ; and every now and then gave her Theatin an amorous ogle, and wantonly pinched his ruddy cheeks. You will at least allow, said Candide to Martin, that these two are a happy couple. Hitherto I have met with none but unfortunate people in the whole habitable globe, except in El Dorado ; but, as to this couple, I would venture to lay a wager they are happy. I will lay you what you please that they are not, said Martin. Well, we have only to ask them to dine with us, said Candide, and you will see whether I am mistaken or not.

Upon this, Candide goes up to them, and with great politeness invites them to his inn to eat some macaroni, with Lombard partridges and caviare, and to drink a bottle of Montepulciano, Lachryma Christi, Cyprus and Samos wine. The girl blushed ; the Theatin accepted the invitation, and she followed him, eyeing Candide every now and then with a mixture of surprise and confusion, while the tears stole down her cheeks. Scarce had she entered his apartment, when she cried out, How, Master Candide, don't you recollect poor Pacquette ? do you not know her again ? Candide, who had not regarded her with any degree of attention before, being wholly occupied with the thoughts of his dear Cunégonde exclaimed, Ah ! is it you, child ? was it you that reduced Dr. Pangloss to that fine condition I saw him in ?

Alas ! Sir, answered Pacquette, it was I that did it, indeed. I find you are acquainted with every thing ; and I have been informed of all the dreadful misfortunes that happened to the whole family of my Lady Baroness and the fair Cunégonde. But I can safely swear to you, that my lot has been no less deplorable ; I was a virtuous girl when you saw me last. A wicked Cordelier, who was my confessor, easily seduced me ; the consequences proved terrible. I was obliged to leave the castle but a little while after the Baron kicked you out ; and if a famous surgeon had not taken compassion on me, I had been a dead woman. Gratitude made me live with him some time as a mistress : his wife, who was a very devil for jealousy, beat me unmercifully every day. Oh ! she was a perfect fury. The doctor himself was the most frightful fellow you ever saw, and surely I was the most wretched creature existing, to be continually beaten for a man whom I did not love. You are not perhaps sensible, Sir, how dangerous it is for an ill-natured woman to be married to a physician. Incensed at the continual bad behaviour of his wife, he one day gave her so effectual a remedy for a slight cold she had caught, that she died in less than two hours in shocking convulsions. Her relations prosecuted the husband, who was obliged to fly, and I was sent to prison. My innocence would not have saved me, if I had not been tolerably handsome. The judge gave me my liberty, on condition he should succeed the doctor. However, I was soon supplanted by a rival, turned off without a farthing, and obliged to continue the abominable trade which you men think so pleasing, but which to us unhappy creatures, is the moſt dreadful of all sufferings. At length I came to follow the business at Venice. Ah! Sir, did you but know what it is to be obliged to lie with every fellow; with old tradesmen, with counsellors, with monks, watermen, and abbés; to be exposed to all their insolence and abuse; to be often necessitated to borrow a petticoat, only that it may be taken up by some disagreeable wretch; to be robbed by one gallant of what we get from another; to be subject to the extortions of civil magiſtrates; and to have for ever before one's eyes the prospect of old age, an hospital, or a dunghill, you would conclude that I am one of the moſt unhappy wretches breathing.

Thus did Pacquette unbosom herself to honeſt Candide in his closet, in the presence of Martin, who took occasion to say to him, You see I have won half of my wager already.

Friar Giroflée was all this time in the dining room refreshing himself with a whet, before dinner was served up. But, said Candide to Pacquette, you looked so gay and content, when I met you, you sung and caressed the Theatin with so much fondness, that I absolutely thought you as happy as you say you are now miserable. Ah! dear Sir, said Pacquette, this is one of the miseries of the trade; yeſterday I was ſtript and beaten by a drunken officer; yet to-day I muſt appear good-humoured and gay to please a monk.

Candide was perfectly satisfied, and acknowledged that Martin was in the right. They sat down to table with Pacquette and the Theatin ; the entertainment was very agreeable and towards the end they began to converse together with mutual confidence. Father, said Candide, to the Friar, you seem to me to enjoy a state of happiness that even kings might envy ; joy and health are painted in your countenance. You have a tight pretty wench to divert you ; and you seem to be perfectly well contented with your condition as a Theatin.

Faith, Sir, said Father Giroflée, I wish the Theatins were every one of them at the bottom of the sea. I have been tempted a thousand times to set fire to the convent and go and turn Turk. My parents obliged me, at the age of fifteen, to put on this detestable habit only to increase the fortune of an elder brother of mine, whom God confound ! Jealousy, discord, and fury, reside in our convent. It is true, I have preached a few paltry sermons, by which I have got a little money, part of which the prior robs me of, and the remainder helps to pay my girls ; but, at night, when I go home to my convent, I am ready to dash my brains against the walls of the dormitory ; and this is the case with all the rest of the brotherhood.

Martin, turning towards Candide, with his usual coolness, said, Well, what think you now ? have I won the wager entirely ? Candide gave two thousand piastres to Pacquette, and a thousand to Friar Giroflée. And now says he, I will

answer for it that this will make them happy.
I don't think so, said Martin; perhaps this
money will only make them more wretched. Be
that as it may, said Candide, one thing comforts
me; I see that one often meets with those whom
we never expected to see again; so that, perhaps,
as I have found my red sheep and Pacquette, I
may be lucky enough to find Mistress Cunégonde. I wish, said Martin, she may ever make
you happy, but I doubt it much. You are very
hard of belief, said Candide. I have seen the
world, said Martin.

Observe those gondoliers, said Candide, are
they not perpetually singing? You do not see
them, answered Martin, at home with their wives
and brats. The doge has his vexations, gondoliers have theirs. Nevertheless, in the main,
I esteem the gondolier's life preferable to that of
the doge; but the difference is so trifling, that
it is not worth the trouble of enquiring into.

I have heard great talk, said Candide, of the
Senator Pococurante, who lives in that fine house
at the Brenta, where, they say, he entertains
foreigners in the most polite manner. They
pretend this man never knew what it was to be
uneasy. I should be glad to see so extraordinary
a being, said Martin. Candide thereupon sent
a messenger to Seignor Pococurante, desiring
permission to visit him the next day.

CHAPTER XXV

Candide and Martin pay a visit to Seignor Poco-curante, a Noble Venetian.

CANDIDE and his friend Martin hired a gondola, and went to the Brenta, and arrived at the palace of the noble Pococurante : the gardens were extensive and laid out in good taste, and adorned with fine marble statues ; his palace was built in a beautiful style of architecture. The master of the house, who was a man of sixty, and very rich, received our two travellers with great civility, but very little ceremony, which somewhat disconcerted Candide, but was not at all displeasing to Martin.

As soon as they were seated, two very pretty girls, neatly dressed, brought in chocolate, which was extremely well frothed. Candide could not help making encomiums upon their beauty, their neat appearance, and attention. They are well enough, said the Senator ; I make them lie with me sometimes, for I am heartily tired of the city ladies, their coquetry, their jealousy, their quarrels, their humours, their meanness, their pride, and their folly ; I am weary of making sonnets, or of paying for sonnets to be made on them ; but, after all, these two girls begin to grow very indifferent to me.

After breakfast, Candide walked into a large gallery, where he was struck with the sight of a number of very excellent paintings. Pray, said Candide, by what master are the two first of these ? They are Raphael's, answered the Senator. I purchased them at a great price, seven years ago, purely out of vanity, as they were said to be the finest pieces in Italy ; but I cannot say they please me : the colouring is dark and heavy ; the figures do not come out enough, they want relief, and the drapery is very bad. In short, notwithstanding the encomiums lavished upon them, they are not, in my opinion, a true representation of nature. To please me I must behold Nature herself in a picture ; and there are none of that kind to be met with. I have a great many paintings, but I do not admire them.

While dinner was getting ready, Pococurante ordered a concert. Candide praised the music to the skies. This noise, said the noble Venetian, may amuse one for half an hour, but if it was to last longer, it would grow tiresome to every body, though perhaps no one would dare to own it. Music is become the art of executing what is difficult ; now, that which has nothing but difficulty to recommend it cannot be long pleasing.

I believe I might take more pleasure in an opera, if they had not made such a monster of it as perfectly shocks me ; let who will go to see wretched tragedies set to music ; where the scenes are contrived for no other purpose than to introduce, oftentimes, very mal-apropos, three

K   123

or four ridiculous songs, to give a favourite actress an opportunity of exhibiting her pipe. Let who will, or can, die away in raptures at the trills of an eunuch quavering the majestic part of Cæsar or Cato, and strutting in a foolish manner upon the stage ; for my part, I have long ago renounced these paltry entertainments, which constitute the glory of modern Italy, and which crowned heads encourage so liberally. Candide opposed these sentiments ; but he did it with caution ; as for Martin, he was entirely of the old Senator's opinion.

Dinner being served up they sat down to table, and, after a very hearty repast, returned to the library. Candide observing Homer richly bound, commended the noble Venetian's taste. This, said he, is a book that was once the delight of the great Pangloss, the best philosopher in Germany. I take no delight in Homer, answered Pococurante, very coolly : I was made to believe once that I took a pleasure in reading him ; but his continual repetitions of battles, which are all alike ; his gods that are always in action, without ever doing any thing ; his Helen, that is the cause of the war, and yet hardly acts in the whole performance ; his Troy, that holds out so long, without being taken ; in short, all these things together make the poem very tiresome to me. I have asked some learned men, whether they are not in reality as much tired as myself with reading this poet : those who spoke ingenuously, assured me that they had sometimes fallen asleep with it in their hands ; and yet, that they could not well avoid giving him a place in their libraries ; but it was merely as they would do an antique, or those rusty medals which are kept only for curiosity, and are of no manner of use as current coin.

But your excellency does not surely form the same opinion of Virgil ? said Candide. Why, I grant, replied Pococurante, that the second, third, fourth, and sixth book of his Æneid are excellent ; but as for his pious Æneas, his strong Cloanthus, his friendly Achates, his boy Ascanius, his silly king Latinus, his ill-bred Amata, and his insipid Lavinia, I think there cannot, in nature, be any thing more flat and disagreeable. I must confess, I prefer Tasso far beyond him ; nay, even that sleepy tale-teller Ariosto.

May I take the liberty to ask if you do not receive great pleasure from reading Horace ? said Candide. There are maxims in this writer, replied Pococurante, from whence a man of the world may reap some benefit ; and the expressive energy of the verse fixes them more easily in the memory. But I see nothing extraordinary in his journey to Brundusium, and his account of his bad dinner ; nor in his dirty low quarrel between one Rupilius, whose words, as he expresses it, were full of poisonous filth ; and another, whose language was dipped in vinegar. His indelicate verses against old women and witches disgusted me exceedingly ; nor can I discover the great merit of his telling his friend

Mecænas, that if he will but rank him in the class of lyric poets, his lofty head shall touch the stars. Ignorant readers are apt to praise every thing by the lump in a writer of reputation. For my part, I read only to please myself. I like nothing but what suits my own taste. Candide, who had been brought up with a notion of never trusting to his own judgment, was astonished at what he had heard ; but Martin found there was a good deal of reason in the Senator's remarks.

O ! here is a Tully, said Candide : this great man, I fancy, you are never tired of reading ? Indeed, I never read him at all, replied Pococurante. What is it to me whether he pleads for Rabirius or Cluentius ? I try causes enough myself. Upon the whole, his philosophical works pleased me most ; but when I found he doubted of every thing, I thought I knew as much as himself, and had no need to a guide to learn ignorance.

Ha ! cried Martin, here are fourscore volumes of the Memoirs of the Academy of Sciences ; perhaps we may find something good in this collection. Yes, answered Pococurante ; so we might if any one of these compilers of this rubbish had only invented the art of pin making : but all these volumes are filled with mere chimerical systems, without one single article of useful information.

What a prodigious number of plays, said Candide, in Italian, Spanish, and French ! Yes, replied the Venetian ; there are I think three thousand, and not three dozen of them good for any thing. As to these huge volumes of divinity, and those enormous collections of sermons, they are not altogether worth one single page in Seneca ; and I fancy you will readily believe that neither myself, nor any one else, ever opens them.

Martin, perceiving some shelves filled with English books, said to the Senator, I fancy that a republican must be highly delighted with those books, which are most of them written with a noble spirit of freedom. It is noble to write as we think, said Pococurante : it is the privilege of humanity. Throughout Italy we write only what we do not think ; and the present inhabitants of the country of the Cæsars and Antoninus's dare not acquire a single idea without the permission of a father dominican. I should be enamoured of the spirit of the English nation, did it not utterly frustrate the good effects it would produce, by passion and the spirit of party.

Candide, seeing a Milton, asked the Senator if he did not think that author a great man ? Who ! said Pococurante sharply ; that barbarian who writes a tedious commentary in ten books of rumbling verse, on the first chapter of Genesis ! that slovenly imitator of the Greeks, who disfigures the creation ; and while Moses represents the Deity as producing the whole universe by his fiat ? makes the Messias take a pair of compasses from the armoury of Heaven, to trace out his intended work ! Can I, think you, have any esteem for a writer who has spoiled Tasso's hell and the devil? who transforms Lucifer sometimes into a toad, and, at others, into a pigmy? who makes him say the same thing over again an hundred times? who makes him a casuist in theology? and who, by an absurdly serious imitation of Ariosto's comic invention of fire-arms, represents the devils and angels, cannonading each other in heaven? Neither I nor any other Italian can possibly take pleasure in such melancholy reveries; but the marriage of Sin and Death, and snakes issuing from the womb of the former, are enough to make any person sick that is not lost to all sense of delicacy. This obscure, whimsical, and disagreeable poem, was slighted at its first publication; and I only treat the author now as he was treated in his own country by his contemporaries. Such are my sentiments, I speak my mind, and am perfectly indifferent, whether others think as I do or not.

Candide was sensibly grieved at this speech, as he had a great respect for Homer, and was very fond of Milton. Alas! said he softly to Martin, I am afraid this man holds our German poets in great contempt. There would be no such great harm in that, said Martin. O, what a surprising man! said Candide still to himself; what a prodigious genius is this Pococurante! nothing can please him.

After finishing their survey of the library, they went down into the garden, when Candide commended the several beauties that offered themselves to his view. It is all in a very bad taste, said Pococurante ; every thing about it is childish and trifling ; but I shall have another laid out to-morrow upon a grander scale.

As soon as our curious visitors had taken leave of his Excellency, Well, said Candide to Martin, I hope you will own, that this man is the happiest of all mortals, for he is above every thing he possesses. But do not you see, answered Martin, that he is disgusted with every thing he possesses ? It was an observation of Plato, long since, that those are not the best stomachs that reject, without distinction, all sorts of food. True, said Candide, but still there must certainly be a pleasure in criticising every thing, and in perceiving faults where others think they see beauties. That is, replied Martin, there is a pleasure in having no pleasure. Well, well, said Candide, I find that I shall be the only happy man at last, when I am blessed with the sight of my dear Cunégonde. It is good to hope, said Martin.

In the mean while, days and weeks passed away, and no news of Cacambo. Candide was so overwhelmed with grief, that he did not reflect on the behaviour of Pacquette and Friar Giroflée, who never staid to return him thanks for the presents he had so generously made them.

CHAPTER XXVI

Candide and Martin sup with six Strangers ; and who they were.

CANDIDE, followed by his friend Martin, was going to sit down to supper one evening, with some travellers who occupied the same inn, when a man, with a face the colour of soot, came behind him, and taking him by the arm, said, Hold yourself in readiness to go along with us, be sure you do not fail. Upon this, turning about, he beheld Cacambo. Nothing but the sight of Mistress Cunégonde could have given him greater joy and surprize. He was almost beside himself. After embracing this dear friend, Cunégonde, said he, Cunégonde is come with you, doubtless ? Where, where is she ? Carry me to her this instant, that I may die with joy in her presence. Cunégonde is not here, answered Cacambo ; she is at Constantinople. Good heavens, at Constantinople ! but what does that signify, if she was in China, I would fly thither. Quick, quick, dear Cacambo, let us be gone. We will go after supper, said Cacambo, I cannot at present stay to say any thing more to you ; I am a slave, and my master waits for me : I must go and attend him at table :

but mum ! say not a word, only get your supper, and hold yourself in readiness.

Candide, divided between joy and grief charmed to have thus met with his faithful agent again, and surprised to hear he was a slave, his heart palpitating, his senses confused, but full of the hopes of recovering his dear Cunégonde, sat down to table with Martin, who beheld all these scenes with great unconcern, and with six strangers who were come to spend the carnival at Venice.

Cacambo was employed in waiting upon one of those strangers. When supper was nearly over, he approached his master, and whispered him in the ear, Sire, your Majesty may go when you please, the ship is ready ; and so saying he went out. The guests, surprised at what they had heard, looked at each other without speaking a word ; when another servant drawing near to his master, in like manner said, Sire, your Majesty's post-chaise is at Padua, and the bark is ready. His master made him a sign, and he instantly withdrew. The company all stared at each other again, and the general astonishment was increased. A third servant then approached another of the strangers, and said, Sire, believe me, your Majesty had better not make any longer stay in this place ; I will go and get every thing ready ; and instantly disappeared.

Candide and Martin then took it for granted, that these were characters in masquerade, it being carnival time. Then a fourth domestic said to the fourth stranger, Your Majesty may set off when you please ; saying this, he went away like the rest. A fifth valet said the same to a fifth master. But the sixth domestic made a different speech to the person on whom he waited, and who sat near to Candide. Troth, Sir, said he, they will trust your Majesty no longer, nor myself neither ; and we may both of us chance to be sent to gaol this very night ; and therefore I shall even take care of myself, and so adieu. The servants being all gone, the six strangers, with Candide and Martin, remained in a profound silence. At length Candide broke it, by saying, Gentlemen, this is very droll, upon my word ; how came you all to be kings ? For my part, I must confess, that neither my friend Martin here nor myself, have any such titles.

Cacambo's master then very gravely answered in Italian : I am not joking in the least, my name is Achmet III. I was Grand Seignor for many years ; I dethroned my brother, my nephew dethroned me, my Viziers were beheaded, and I am condemned to end my days in the old Seraglio. My nephew, the Grand Sultan Mahomet, gives me permission to travel sometimes for my health, and I am come to spend the carnival at Venice.

A young man who sat by Achmet spoke next, and said, My name is Ivan. I was once Emperor of all the Russias, but was dethroned in my cradle. My father and mother were imprisoned, and I was brought up in a prison ; yet

I am sometimes allowed to travel, though always with persons to keep a guard over me, and I am come to spend the carnival at Venice.

The third said, I am Charles Edward, King of England ; my father abdicated the throne in my favour. I have fought in defence of my rights, and near a thousand of my friends have had their hearts torn out of their bodies, and thrown in their faces. I have myself been confined in a prison. I am going to Rome to visit the King my father, who was dethroned as well as myself and my grandfather ; and I am come to spend the carnival at Venice.

The fourth spoke thus, I am the King of Poland ; the fortune of war has stripped me of my hereditary dominions. My father experienced the same reverse of fortune. I resign myself to the will of Providence, like Sultan Achmet, the Emperor Ivan, and King Charles Edward, whom God long preserve ; and I am come to spend the carnival at Venice.

The fifth said, I am King of Poland also. I have twice lost my kingdom ; but Providence has given me a different establishment, where I have done more good than all the Sarmatian Kings, put together, were ever able to do on the banks of the Vistula : I resign myself likewise to Providence ; and am come to spend the carnival at Venice.

It now came to the sixth Monarch's turn to speak. Gentlemen, said he, I am not so great a prince as the rest of you, it is true ; but I am, however, a crowned head. I am Theodore, elected King of Corsica. I have had the title of Majesty, and am now scarcely treated like a gentleman. I have coined money, and am now not worth a farthing. I have had two Secretaries of State, and am now without a single valet. I was once seated on a throne, and since that have lain upon a truss of straw, in a common gaol in London, and I very much fear I shall meet with the same fate here in Venice, where I come, like your Majesties, to divert myself at the carnival. The other five kings listened to this speech with great attention ; it excited their compassion ; each of them made the unhappy Theodore a present of twenty sequins, to buy him a few shirts and some better cloaths ; and Candide gave him a diamond worth two thousand sequins. Who can this private person be, said the five princes to one another, who is able to give, and has given, an hundred times as much as any of us ?

Just as they rose from table, in came four Serene Highnesses, who had also been stripped of their territories by the fortune of war, and were come to spend the remainder of the carnival at Venice. But Candide took no manner of notice of them ; for his thoughts were wholly employed on his voyage to Constantinople, whither he intended to go in search of his lovely Mistress Cunégonde.

CHAPTER XXVII

Candide's Voyage to Constantinople.

THE faithful Cacambo had already prevailed upon the captain of the Turkish ship, that was to carry Sultan Achmet back to Constantinople, to take Candide and Martin on board. Accordingly they both embarked, after paying their obeisance to his unfortunate Highness. As they were going on board, Candide said to Martin, You see how the world goes, we supped in company with six dethroned kings, and one of them was so poor that I gave him charity. Perhaps there may be a great many other princes still more unfortunate. For my part, I have lost only an hundred sheep, and am now going to fly to the arms of my charming Mistress Cunégonde. My dear Martin, I must still insist on it, that Pangloss was in the right. All is for the best. I wish it may, said Martin.—But this was certainly a very improbable adventure, which we met with at Venice. I do not think that any one ever saw or heard of six dethroned monarchs supping together at a public inn. This is not more extraordinary, said Martin, than most of the things that have happened to us. It is a very common thing for kings to be dethroned ; and

135

as for our having the honour to sup with six of them, it is a mere trifle, not worth remarking.

As soon as Candide set his foot on board the vessel, he flew to his old friend and valet Cacambo ; and, throwing his arms about his neck, embraced him with transports of joy. Well, said he, what news of Mistress Cunégonde ? Does she still continue the paragon of beauty ? Does she love me still ? How does she do ? You have, doubtless, purchased a palace for her at Constantinople.

My dear master, replied Cacambo, Mistress Cunégonde washes dishes on the banks of the Propontis, in the house of a prince who has very few to wash. She is at present a slave in the family of an ancient sovereign, named Ragotsky, whom the Grand Turk allows three crowns a day to maintain him in his exile ; but the worst part of the story is, that she is grown horribly ugly. Ugly, or handsome, said Candide, I am a man of honour ; and, as such, am obliged to love her still. But how could she possibly have been reduced to so abject a condition, when I sent five or six millions to her by you ? Very true, said Cacambo, but was not I obliged to give two millions to Seignior Don Fernando d'Ibaraa y Figueora y Mascarenes y Lampourdos y Souza, the Governor of Buenos Ayres, for liberty to take Mistress Cunégonde away with me ? and then did not a brave fellow of a pirate very gallantly strip us of all the rest ? and then did not this same pirate carry us with him to Cape

136

Matapan, to Milo, to Nicaria, to Samos, to Petra, to the Dardanelles, to Marmora, to Scutari? Mistress Cunégonde and the old woman are now servants to the Prince I have told you of ; and I myself am slave to the dethroned Sultan. What a chain of shocking accidents ! exclaimed Candide. But, after all, I have still some diamonds left, with which I can easily procure Mistress Cunégonde's liberty. It is a pity she is grown so very ugly.

Then, turning his discourse to Martin, What think you, friend, said he, whose condition is most to be pitied, the Emperor Achmet's, the Emperor Ivan's, King Charles Edward's, or mine ? Faith, I cannot resolve your question, said Martin, unless I had been in all your hearts, and knew all your feelings. Ah ! cried Candide, was Pangloss here now, he would have known, and satisfied me at once. I know not, said Martin, in what balance your Pangloss could have weighed the misfortunes of mankind, and have set a just estimation on their sufferings. All that I know is, that there are millions of men on the earth, whose conditions are an hundred times more pitiable than those of King Charles Edward, the Emperor Ivan, or Sultan Achmet. Why, that may be, answered Candide.

In a few days they reached the Black Sea ; and Candide began by paying an extravagant ransom for Cacambo : then, without losing time, he and his companions went on board a galley, in order to search for his Cunégonde, on the banks of the Propontis, notwithstanding she was grown so ugly.

There were two slaves among the crew of the galley, who rowed very awkwardly, and to whose bare backs the master of the vessel frequently applied a bull's pizzle. Candide, from natural sympathy, looked at these two slaves more attentively than at any of the rest, and drew near them with an eye of pity. Their features, though greatly disfigured, appeared to him to have some resemblance with those of Pangloss and the unhappy Baron Jesuit, Mistress Cunégonde's brother. This idea affected him with grief and compassion : he examined them more attentively than before. In troth, said he, turning to Cacambo, if I had not seen my master Pangloss fairly hanged, and had not myself been unlucky enough to run the Baron through the body, I should absolutely think those two rowers were the men.

The names of the Baron and Pangloss were no sooner heard than the two slaves gave a great cry, ceased rowing, and let fall their oars out of their hands. The master of the vessel, seeing this, ran up to them, and redoubled the discipline of the bull's pizzle. Hold, hold, cried Candide, I will give you what money you shall ask for these two persons. Good heavens ! it is Candide, said one of the men. Candide ! cried the other. Do I dream, said Candide, or am I awake ? Am I actually on board this galley ? Is this my Lord Baron, whom I killed ? and that my master Pangloss, whom I saw hanged before my face?

The same, the same! cried they both together. What? is this your great philosopher? said Martin. My dear Sir, said Candide to the master of the galley, how much do you ask for the ransom of the Baron of Thunder-ten-Tronckh, who is one of the first Barons of the Empire, and of Dr. Pangloss, the most profound metaphysician in Germany? Why then, Christian cur, replied the Turkish captain, since these two dogs of Christian slaves are Barons and metaphysicians, who no doubt are of high rank in their own country, thou shalt give me fifty thousand sequins. You shall have them, Sir: carry me back as quick as thought to Constantinople, and you shall receive the money immediately—No! carry me first to Mistress Cunégonde. The captain, upon Candide's first proposal, had already tacked about, and he made the crew apply their oars so effectually, that the vessel flew through the water quicker than a bird cleaves the air.

Candide embraced the Baron and Pangloss again and again. And how was it, my dear Baron, I did not kill you? and you, my dear Pangloss, how are you come to life again, after your hanging? And, how came you slaves on board a Turkish galley? And is it true that my dear sister is in this country? said the Baron. Yes, said Cacambo. And do I once again behold my dear Candide? said Pangloss. Candide

L   139

presented Martin and Cacambo to them ; they embraced each other over and over again, and all spoke together. The galley flew like lightning, and now they were got back to the port. Candide instantly sent for a Jew, to whom he sold for fifty thousand sequins a diamond richly worth one hundred thousand, though the fellow swore to him all the time, by father Abraham, that he gave him the most he could possibly afford. He paid it down instantly, for the ransom of the Baron and Pangloss. The latter flung himself at the feet of his deliverer, and bathed them with his tears : The former thanked him like a Baron of the Empire, with a gracious nod, and promised to return him the money the first opportunity. —But is it possible, said he, that my sister should be in Turkey ? Nothing is more possible, answered Cacambo ; for she scours the dishes in the house of a Transylvanian Prince. Candide sent directly for two other Jews, and sold more diamonds to them ; and then he set out with his companions in another galley, to deliver Mistress Cunégonde from slavery.

CHAPTER XXVIII

What befel Candide, Cunégonde, Pangloss, Martin, &c.

PARDON once more, said Candide to the Baron; once more let me intreat you to forgive me, Reverend Father, for running you through the body. Let's forget it, and say no more about it, replied the Baron; I was a little too hasty I must own : but as you seem to be desirous to know by what accident I came to be a slave on board the galley where you saw me, I will inform you. After I had been cured of the wound you gave me, by the college apothecary, I was attacked and carried off by a party of Spanish troops, who clapped me up in prison in Buenos Ayres, at the very time my sister was leaving the place. I asked leave to return to Rome, to the General of my order, who appointed me chaplain to the French Ambassador at Constantinople. I had not been a week in my new office, when I happened to meet one evening with a young Icoglan, extremely handsome and well made. The weather was very hot ; the young man had an inclination to bathe. I took the opportunity to bathe likewise. I did not know it was a capital crime for a Christian to be found naked in company with a young Mussulman.

A Cadi ordered me to receive an hundred blows on the soles of my feet, and sent me to the gallies. I do not believe that there was ever an act of more flagrant injustice. But I would fain know how my sister came to be a scullion to a Transylvanian Prince, who has taken refuge among the Turks?

But by what miracle do I behold you again, my dear Pangloss? said Candide. It is true, answered Pangloss, you saw me hanged, though I ought properly to have been burnt; but you may remember, that it rained extremely hard when they were going to roast me. The storm was so violent, that they found it impossible to light the fire; so they even hanged me, because they could do no better. A surgeon purchased my body, carried it home, and prepared to dissect me. He began by making a crucial incision from my navel to the clavicle. It is impossible for any one to have been more clumsily hanged than I had been. The executioner of the holy inquisition was a sub-deacon, and was an excellent hand at burning people, but as for hanging, he was not used to it; the cord being wet, and not slipping properly, the noose was not tight. In short, I still continued to breathe; the crucial incision made me roar out so loud, that my surgeon fell flat upon his back; and imagining it was the devil he was dissecting, ran away, half dead with fear, and in his fright tumbled down on the staircase. His wife hearing the noise, flew from the next room, and seeing me stretched upon the table with my crucial incision, was still more terrified than her husband, ran away, and fell over him. When they had a little recovered themselves, I heard her say to her husband, My dear, how could you think of dissecting an heretic? Don't you know, that the devil is always in their bodies? I'll run directly to a priest to come and exorcise him. I trembled from head to foot at hearing her talk in this manner, and exerted what little strength I had left to cry out, For God's sake take pity of me! At length the Portuguese barber took courage, sewed up my wound, and his wife nursed me; and I was upon my legs in a fortnight's time. The barber got me a place to be a lacquey to a knight of Malta, who was going to Venice; but finding my master had no money to pay me my wages, I entered into the service of a Venetian merchant, and went with him to Constantinople.

One day I happened to enter a mosque, where I saw no one but an old Iman and a very pretty young female devotee, who was saying her Paternoster; her neck was quite bare, and in her bosom she had a beautiful nosegay of tulips, roses, anemones, ranunculuses, hyacinths, and auriculas. She let fall her nosegay. I ran immediately to take it up, with a most respectful assiduity. But I was so long in putting it in its place, that the Iman began to be angry; and, perceiving I was a Christian, he cried out for help; they carried me before the Cadi, who ordered me to receive one hundred bastinadoes, and sent me to the gallies. I was chained in the very galley, and to the very same bench with the Baron. On board this galley there were four young men belonging to Marseilles, five Neapolitan priests, and two Monks of Corfu, who told us that the like adventures happened every day. The Baron pretended that he had been much more unjustly punished than myself; but I insisted that there was far less harm in taking up a nosegay, and putting it into a woman's bosom, than to be found stark naked with a young Icoglan. We were continually disputing this point, and received twenty lashes a-day with a bull's pizzle, when the concatenation of sublunary events brought you on board our galley to ransom us from slavery.

Well, my dear Pangloss, said Candide to them, when you was hanged, dissected, whipped, and tugging at the oar in the galley, did you continue to think, that every thing in the world happens for the best? I have always retained my first opinion, answered Pangloss; besides, I am a philosopher; and it would not become me to retract my sentiments; especially as Leibnitz could not be in the wrong, and the doctrine of pre-established harmony is the finest thing in the world, as well as a *plenum*, and the *materia subtilis*.

CHAPTER XXIX

*In what Manner Candide found Mistress Cuné-
gonde and the Old Woman again.*

WHILE Candide, the Baron, Pangloss, Martin,
and Cacambo, passed away the time in relating
their several adventures, and reasoning on the
contingent or non contingent events of this
world ; while they disputed on the cause and
effects, on moral and physical evil ; on free-will
and necessity ; and on the many consolations
that may be felt by a person when a slave, and
chained to an oar in a Turkish galley, they arrived
at the house of the Transylvanian Prince, on the
coast of Propontis. The first objects they beheld there was Mistress Cunégonde and the old
woman, who were hanging some table cloths on
a line to dry.

The Baron turned pale at the sight. Even
Candide, that tender and affectionate lover, upon
seeing his fair Cunégonde all sun-burnt, with
blear-eyes, a withered neck, and her arms all
covered with a red scurf, started back with
horror ; but, recovering himself, he advanced
towards her out of good manners, she embraced
Candide and her brother ; they embraced the
old woman, and Candide ransomed them both.

There was a small farm in the neighbourhood,

which the old woman proposed to Candide to rent for the present, till the company should meet with a more agreeable situation. Cunégonde knew nothing of her being grown ugly, as no one had informed her of it, and therefore reminded Candide of his promise, in so peremptory a manner, that the simple lad did not dare to refuse her ; he then acquainted the Baron that he was going to marry his sister. I will never suffer, said the Baron, my sister to be guilty of such meanness on her part ; nor will I bear this insolence on your's : no, I never will be reproached with such a disgrace. My sister's children could not enjoy the ecclesiastical dignities in Germany ; nor shall a sister of mine ever be the wife of any person below the rank of a Baron of the Empire. Cunégonde flung herself at her brother's feet, and bedewed them with her tears, but he still remained inflexible. Silly fellow, said Candide, have I not delivered thee from the gallies, paid thy ransom, and thy sister's too, who was a dish-washer, and is very ugly ? and yet I condescend to marry her ; and shalt thou pretend to oppose the match ? If I were to follow the dictates of a just resentment I should kill thee again. Thou mayest kill me again, said the Baron, but thou shalt not marry my sister while I am living.

CHAPTER XXX

Conclusion.

CANDIDE, in the bottom of his heart, had no great stomach to the match with Mistress Cunégonde ; but the extreme impertinence of the Baron determined him to have her ; and Cunégonde pressed him so warmly, that he could not recant. He consulted Pangloss, Martin, and the faithful Cacambo. Pangloss drew up a fine memorial, by which he proved that the Baron had no right over his sister ; and that she might, even according to all the laws of the empire, marry Candide with the left hand. Martin thought it best to throw the Baron into the sea : Cacambo decided that he must be delivered to the Turkish Captain, and sent to the gallies, after which he should be conveyed by the first ship to the Father-general at Rome. This advice was found to be very good ; the old woman approved of it, but not a word of it was told to his sister ; the business was executed for a little money, and they had the double pleasure of tricking a Jesuit, and punishing the pride of a German Baron.

It is natural enough for the reader to imagine, that, after undergoing so many disasters, Candide, married to his mistress, and living with the philosopher Pangloss, the philosopher Martin, the prudent Cacambo, and the old woman, having besides brought home so many diamonds from the country of the ancient Incas, would lead the most agreeable life in the world. But he had been so much cheated by the Jews, that he had nothing else left but his little farm ; his wife, every day growing more and more ugly, became soured in her temper and insupportable ; the old woman was infirm, and still more ill-natured than Cunégonde. Cacambo, who worked in the garden, and carried the produce of it to sell at Constantinople, was past his labour, and cursed his fate. Pangloss was mortified that he made no figure in any of the German universities. And as to Martin, he was firmly persuaded, that a person is equally ill-situated every where. He bore all with patience. Candide, Martin, and Pangloss, disputed sometimes about metaphysics and morality. Boats were often seen passing under the windows of the farm, fraught with effendis, bashaws, and cadies, that were going into banishment to Lemnos, Mitilene, and Erzerum. And other cadies, bashaws, and effendis, were seen coming back to succeed the place of those who had been banished, and were banished in their turns. They saw several heads very neatly fixed upon poles, and carrying as presents to the Sublime Porte. Such sights gave occasion to frequent dissertations ; and when they had nothing to dispute about, the irksomeness was so excessive, that the old woman ventured one day to tell them, I would be glad to know, which

is worst, to be ravished a hundred times by negro
pirates, to have one buttock cut off, to run the
gantlet among the Bulgarians, to be whipt and
hanged at an Auto-da-fé, to be dissected, to be
chained to an oar in a galley, and in short, to
experience all the miseries through which every
one of us hath passed,—or to remain here doing
of nothing ? This, said Candide, is a very deep
question.

This enquiry gave birth to new reflections, and
Martin, at last, decided, that man was not born
to live in the convulsions of disquiet, or in the
lethargy of idleness. Though Candide was not
entirely of this opinion ; yet he did not determine
any thing on the head. Pangloss confessed that
he had undergone dreadful sufferings ; but
having once maintained that every thing was
perfectly right, he still maintained it, but at the
same time he believed nothing of it.

There was one thing which, more than ever,
confirmed Martin in his detestable principle,
made Candide hesitate, and embarrassed Pangloss—which was, the arrival of Pacquette and
brother Giroflée one day at their farm, in the
utmost distress ; they had very speedily made
away with their three thousand piastres ; they
had parted, been reconciled ; had quarrelled
again, and been thrown into prison ; had made
their escape, and, at last brother Giroflée turned
Turk. Pacquette still continued to follow her
trade wherever she came ; but she got little or
nothing by it. I foresaw very plainly, says

Martin to Candide, that your presents, to this couple, would soon be squandered, and only make them more miserable. You and Cacambo have spent millions of piastres, and yet you are not more happy than brother Giroflée and Pacquette. So! says Pangloss to Pacquette, Heaven has brought you here among us again, my poor child! Do you know that you have cost me the tip of my nose, one eye, and one ear? What a miserable state are you now in! and what is this world! This new adventure engaged them more deeply than ever in philosophical disputations.

There lived in their neighbourhood, a very famous dervise, who passed for the best philosopher in Turkey; they wished to know his opinions: Pangloss, who was their spokesman, addressed him thus, Master, we come to intreat you to tell us, why so strange an animal as man has been formed?

Why do you meddle with the subject? said the dervise; is it any business of your's? But, my Reverend Father, says Candide, there is a horrible deal of evil on the earth. What signifies it, says the dervise, whether there is evil or good? When his Highness sends a ship to Egypt, does he trouble his head, whether the rats in the vessel are at their ease or not? What must then be done? says Pangloss. Be silent; answers the dervise. I flattered myself, replied Pangloss, to have reasoned a little with you on the causes and effects, on the best of possible worlds, the origin of evil, the nature of the soul, and a pre-established harmony. At these words the dervise shut the door in their faces.

During this conversation, news was spread abroad, that two Viziers of the Bench and the Mufti had been just strangled at Constantinople, and several of their friends empaled. This catastrophe made a great noise for some hours. Pangloss, Candide, and Martin, as they were returning to their little farm, met with a good-looking old man, who was taking the air at his door, under an arbour formed of the boughs of orange-trees. Pangloss, who was as inquisitive as he was disputative, asked him what was the name of the Mufti who was lately strangled. I cannot tell, answered the good old man; I never knew the name of any Mufti or Vizier in my life, nor do I know any thing of the event you speak of; I presume, that in general, such as meddle with politics sometimes come to a miserable end; and that they deserve it: but I never enquire what is doing at Constantinople; I am contented with sending thither the fruits of my garden, which I cultivate with my own hands. After saying these words, he invited the strangers to come into his house. His two daughters and two sons presented them with divers sorts of sherbet of their own making; besides caymac, heightened with the peels of candied citrons, oranges, lemons, pine-apples, pistachio-nuts, and Mocha coffee, unadulterated with the bad coffee of Batavia, or the American islands. After which the two daughters of this good Mussulman perfumed the beards of Candide, Pangloss, and Martin.

You must certainly have a vast estate, said Candide to the Turk ; I have no more than twenty acres of ground, said he, the whole of which I cultivate myself with the help of my children ; and by our labour we avoid three great evils, idleness, vice, and want.

Candide, as he was returning home, made profound reflections on the Turk's discourse. This good old man, said Pangloss to Martin, appears to me to have chosen for himself a lot much preferable to that of the six kings, with whom we had the honour to sup. Elevated stations, said Pangloss, are very dangerous, according to the testimonies of almost all philosophers ; for we find Eglon, King of Moab, was assassinated by Aod ; Absalom was hanged by the hair of his head, and run through with three darts ; King Nadab, son of Jeroboam, was slain by Baaza ; King Ela by Zimri ; Okosias by Jehu ; Athaliah by Jehoiada ; the Kings Jehoiakim, Jeconiah, and Zedekiah, were led into captivity : I need not tell you what was the fate of Croesus, Astyages, Darius, Dionysius of Syracuse, Pyrrhus, Perseus, Hannibal, Jugurtha, Ariovistus, Cæsar, Pompey, Nero, Otho, Vitellius, Domitian, Richard II. of England, Edward II., Henry VI., Richard III., Mary Stuart, Charles I., the three Henries of France, and the Emperor Henry IV.; you know also——I know, said Candide, that we must cultivate our garden.

You are in the right, said Pangloss ; for when man was put into the garden of Eden, it was with an intent to dress it : and this proves that man was not born to be idle. Let us work then without cavilling, said Martin ; it is the only way to render life supportable.

The little society, one and all, entered into this laudable design ; and set themselves to exert their different talents. The piece of ground, though small, yielded them a plentiful crop. Cunégonde, indeed, was very ugly, but she became an excellent pastry-cook ; Pacquette embroidered ; the old woman had the care of the linen. There was not one, down to brother Giroflée, but was of some use ; he was a very good carpenter, and became an honest man. Pangloss used now and then to say to Candide, There is certainly a concatenation of all events in the best of possible worlds ; for, in short, had you not been kicked out of that fine castle for the love of Mistress Cunégonde ; had you not been put into the inquisition ; had you not travelled over America on foot ; had you not run the Baron through the body ; and had you not lost all your sheep, which you brought from the good country of El Dorado, you would not have been here to eat preserved citrons and pistachio nuts. All this is excellently observed, answered Candide ; but let us cultivate our garden.

END OF THE FIRST PART.

PART II.

It was thought that Dr. Ralph had no intention to carry on his Treatise of Optimism any further; and therefore it was translated and published as a complete piece; but Dr. Ralph, spirited up by the little cabals of the German universities, added a second part, which we have caused to be translated, to satisfy the impatience of the public, and especially of such who are diverted with the witticisms of Master Alibron, who know what a Merry Andrew is, and who never read the JOURNAL of TREVOUX.

CANDIDE: OR, ALL FOR THE BEST

CHAPTER I

How Candide quitted his Companions, and what happened to him.

IT is one of the imperfections of humanity, that we soon become tired of every thing in life; riches oftentimes harass and teize the possessor; ambition, when once satisfied, leaves only remorse behind it; the joys of love are of short duration; and Candide, made to experience all the vicissitudes of fortune, was soon tired of cultivating his garden. Master Pangloss, said he, if we are in the best possible worlds, you will confess, at least, that this is not enjoying a proper share of possible happiness ; to live unknown, in a little corner of the Propontis, with no other resource than that of my own manual labour, which may one day fail me ; no other pleasures than what Miſtress Cunégonde gives me, who is very ugly : and, which is worse, is my wife ; no other company than your's, which is sometimes tiresome, or that of Martin, which gives me the spleen, or that of Giroflée, who is but very lately become an honeſt man ; or that of Pacquette, the danger of whose correspondence you have so fully experienced : or that of the old woman who has but one buttock, and is conſtantly repeating old ſtories which sets one asleep.

To this Pangloss made the following reply : Philosophy teaches us, that Monads divisible *in infinitum*, arrange themselves with wonderful sagacity, in order to compose the different bodies which we observe in nature. The heavenly bodies are what they ought to be ; they are placed where they should be ; they describe the circles which they ought to do ; man follows the bent he ought to follow ; he is what he ought to be ; he does what he ought to do. You bemoan yourself, O Candide ! because the Monad of your soul is disguſted : but disguſt is a modification of the soul ; and this does not hinder, but every thing is for the beſt, both for you and others. When you beheld me covered with ulcers, it did not alter my opinion ; for if Pacquette had not made me taſte the pleasures of love and its poison, I should not have met with you in Holland ; I should not have given the anabaptist James an opportunity of performing a worthy action ; I should not have been hanged in Lisbon for the edification of my neighbour ; I should not have been here to assist you with my advice, and make you live and die in Leibnitz's opinion. Yes, my dear Candide, every thing is linked in a chain, every thing is necessary in the best of possible worlds. There is a necessity that the Burgher of Montauban should instruct kings ; that the worm of Quimper-Corentin should carp, carp, carp ; that the declaimer against philosophers should occasion his own crucifixion in St. Denis street ; that a rascally Recollet, and the Archdeacon of St. Malo, should diffuse their gall and calumny through their Christian Journals ; that philosophy should be accused at the tribunal of Melpomene ; and that philosophers should continue to enlighten human nature, notwithstanding the croakings of ridiculous animals that flounder in the marshes of learning : and should you be once more driven by a hearty kicking from the finest of all castles, to learn again your exercise among the Bulgarians ; should you again suffer the dirty effects of a Dutch-woman's zeal ; be half-drowned again before Lisbon ; be unmercifully whipped again by order of the most holy inquisition ; should you run the same risks again among Los Padres, the Oreillons, and the French ; should you, in short, suffer every misfortune possible, and never understand Leibnitz better than I myself do, you will still maintain that every thing is right ; that all is for the best ; that a *plenum*, the *materia subtilis*, a pre-established harmony, and Monads, are the finest things in the world ; and that Leibnitz is a great man, even to those who do not comprehend him.

To this fine speech, Candide, the mildest being in nature, though he had killed three men, two of whom were priests, answered not a word : but quite tired of the doctor and his society, next morning, at break of day, taking a white staff in his hand, he set off, without knowing what route he should take, but in quest of a place, if to be found, where one does not become tired of one's situation, and where men are not men, as in the good country of El Dorado.

Candide, so much the less unhappy, as he was no longer in love with Mistress Cunégonde, living upon the bounty of different people, who are not Christians, but yet are charitable, arrived, after a very long and very tiresome journey on foot, at Tauris upon the frontiers of Persia, a city noted for the cruelties which the Turks and Persians have by turns exercised therein.

Exhausted with fatigue, with scarcely more clothes than what were necessary to cover that part which constitutes the man, and which men call shameful, Candide was almost ready to give up Pangloss's opinion, when a Persian accosted him in the most polite manner, beseeching him to ennoble his house with his presence. You are laughing at me, says Candide to him ; I am a poor devil, who have left a miserable cottage I had in Propontis, because I had married Mistress Cunégonde ; because she is grown very ugly, and because I was tired of my life ; I am not, indeed, made to ennoble any body's house ; I am not noble myself, thank God : If I had the honour of being so, Baron Thunder-ten-Tronchk should have paid very dear when he favoured me with so many kicks on the breech, or I should have died of shame for it, which would have been pretty philosophical : besides, I have been whipt very ignominiously by the executioners of the most holy inquisition, and by two thousand heroes, at three-pence half-penny a-day. Give me what you please, but do not insult my distress with railleries, which would take away all the merit of your beneficence. My Lord, replied the Persian, you may be a beggar, and indeed your appearance has much the look of it ; but my religion obliges me to use hospitality : it is sufficient that you are a man, and under misfortunes, that the apple of my eye should be the path for your feet ; vouchsafe to ennoble my house with your radiant presence. I will, since you insist upon it, answered Candide. Come then, enter, says the Persian. They went in accordingly, and Candide was all astonishment at the respectful treatment shewn him by his host. The slaves prevented his desires ; the whole house seemed to be busied in nothing but making him welcome. If this does but last, said Candide to himself, all does not go so badly in this country. Three days were past, during which time the kind attentions of the Persian continued the same as at first; and Candide already cried out, Master Pangloss, I always imagined you were in the right, for you are a great philosopher.

CHAPTER II

What befel Candide in this House; and how he got out of it.

CANDIDE, now lived well, was well drest, and had nothing to vex him, so that he soon became as ruddy, as fresh, and as gay, as he had been at Westphalia. His host, Ismael Raab, was delighted with this change : he was a man six feet high, adorned with two small eyes, extremely red, and a large carbuncled nose, which sufficiently declared his infraction of Mahomet's law : his whiskers were celebrated throughout the country, and mothers wished their sons nothing more than such a pair. Raab had wives, because he was rich : but he thought in a manner that is but too common in the East, and in some parts of Italy. Your Excellence is more beautiful than the stars, says one day the artful Persian to the simple Candide, gently stroking his chin ; you must have

captivated a great many hearts : you are formed
to give and receive happiness. Alas ! answered
our hero, I was but half happy once behind a
screen, where I was but aukwardly situated with
Mademoiselle Cunégonde. She was handsome
then——Mademoiselle Cunégonde ! said the
Persian, poor innocent thing ! Follow me, my
Lord ; and Candide followed accordingly. They
came to a very agreeable retreat, where silence
and pleasure reigned. There Ismael Raab
amorously embraced Candide, and in a few
words made a declaration of love like that which
the beautiful Alexis expresses with so much
pleasure in Virgil's Eclogues. Candide was
petrified with aſtonishment. No ; cried he, I
can never suffer such infamy ! what a cause, and
what horrible effect ! I had rather die. So you
shall then says Ismael enraged : how, thou
Chriſtian dog ! because I would politely give
you pleasure—resolve directly to satisfy me, or
to suffer the moſt cruel death. Candide did
not long hesitate. The cogent reason of the
Persian made him tremble, for he feared death
as every philosopher should.

We accuſtom ourselves to every thing in time.
Candide, well fed, well taken care of, but always
closely watched, was not absolutely disguſted
with his condition. Good cheer, and the different
diversions performed by Ismael's slaves, gave
some relief to his chagrin : he was unhappy only
when he reflected ; and that's the case with the
greateſt part of mankind.

At that time, one of the most staunch supporters of the monkish crew in Persia the most learned of the Mahometan doctors, who understood Arabic perfectly, and even Greek, as spoken at this day in the country of Demosthenes and Sophocles, the reverend Ed-Ivan-Baal-Denk, returned from Constantinople, where he had conversed with the Reverend Mamoud-Abram on a very delicate point of doctrine ; namely, whether the prophet had plucked from the angel Gabriel's wing the pen which he used for the writing of the Alcoran ; or, if Gabriel had made him a present of it. They had disputed for three days and three nights with a warmth worthy of the noblest ages of controversy ; and the doctor returned home, persuaded, like all the disciples of Ali, that Mahomet had plucked the quill ; while Mamoud-Abram remained convinced, like the rest of Omar's followers, that the Prophet was incapable of committing any such rudeness, and that the angel had made him a present of this quill for his pen, with all the politeness imaginable.

It is said that there was at Constantinople a certain free-thinker, who insinuated that it would be proper to examine first whether the Alcoran was really written with a pen taken from the wing of the angel Gabriel ; but he was stoned.

Candide's arrival had made a noise in Tauris : many who had heard him speak of contingent and non-contingent effects, imagined he was a philosopher. There were some who mentioned him

to Ed-Ivan-Baal-Denk ; he had the curiosity
to come and see him ; and Raab, who could
hardly refuse a person of such consequence, sent
for Candide to make his appearance. He seemed
to be well pleased with the manner in which
Candide spake of physical evil, and moral evil,
of agent and actuated. I understand that you
are a philosopher, and that's sufficient, said the
venerable Recluse : It is not right, that so great
a man as you are should be treated with such
indignity, as I am told, in the world. You are
a foreigner, Ismael Raab has no right over you.
I propose to introduce you at court ; there you
shall meet with a favourable reception : the
Sophi loves the sciences. Ismael, you must
put this young philosopher into my hands, or
dread incurring the displeasure of the Prince,
and drawing upon yourself the vengeance of
Heaven ; but especially of the monks. These
last words terrified the bold Persian, and he consented to every thing : Candide, blessing Heaven
and the monks, went the same day out of Tauris,
with the Mahometan doctor. They took the
road to Ispahan, where they arrived loaded with
the blessings and favours of the people.

CHAPTER III

Candide's Reception at Court, and what followed.

THE Reverend Ed-Ivan-Baal-Denk was not long before he presented Candide to the King. His Majesty took a particular pleasure in hearing him : he made him dispute with several learned men of his Court, and treated him like a fool, an ignoramus, and idiot ; which very much contributed to persuade his Majesty, that he was a great man. Because, said he to them, you do not comprehend Candide's reasonings, you talk nonsense to him ; but I, who understand them as little, assure you that he is a great philosopher, and I swear it by my whisker. Upon these words, the literati were struck dumb.

Candide was lodged in the palace ; he had slaves to wait on him ; he was dressed in magnificent cloaths, and the Sophi commanded, that whatever he should say, no one should dare to attempt to prove him in the wrong. His Majesty did not stop here. The venerable Monk was continually soliciting him in favour of his guest, and his Majesty, at length, resolved to rank him among the number of his most intimate favourites.

God be praised, and our holy Prophet, says the Iman, addressing himself to Candide ; I am come to tell you a very agreeable piece of news ; How happy you are, my dear Candide ; How many will be jealous of you ! you shall swim in opulence ; you may aspire to the most splendid posts in the Empire. But do not forget me, my friend : think that it is I who have procured you the favour, you are just upon the point of enjoying : let gaiety reign over the horizon of your countenance. The King grants you a favour, which numbers have wished for, and you will soon exhibit a sight which the court has not enjoyed these two years past. And what are these favours, demanded Candide, with which the Prince intends to honour me ? This very day, answered the Monk, quite overjoyed, this very day you are to receive fifty strokes with a bull's pizzle on the soles of your feet, in the presence of his Majesty. The eunuchs appointed to perfume you for the occasion are to be here directly ; prepare yourself to go cheerfully through this little trial, and thereby render yourself worthy of the King of Kings. Let the King of Kings, cried Candide in a rage, keep his favours to himself, if I must receive fifty blows with a bull's pizzle, in order to merit them. It is thus, replied the doctor drily, that he deals with those on whom he means to pour down his benefits. I love you too much to regard the little pet which you show on the occasion, and I will make you happy in spite of yourself.

He had scarce done speaking, when the eunuchs arrived, preceded by the executor of his

Majesty's private pleasures, who was one of the greatest and most robust Lords of the court. Candide said and did all he could, but in vain. They perfumed his legs and feet, according to custom. Four eunuchs carried him to the place appointed for the ceremony, through the midst of a double file of soldiers, while the trumpets sounded, the cannon fired, and the bells of all the mosques of Ispahan were ringing : the Sophi was already there, accompanied by his principal officers and people of the first quality in his court. In an instant they stretched out Candide upon a little form, finely gilt, and the executor of the private pleasures began to prepare himself for the business. O ! Master Pangloss, Master Pangloss, were you but here !—said Candide, weeping and roaring out as loud as he could bawl ; a circumstance which would have been thought very indecent, if the monk had not given the people to understand, that his guest acted in this manner, only the better to divert his Majesty. This great king, it is true, laughed like any idiot: he even took such delight in the affair, that after the fifty blows had been given, he ordered him fifty more. But his first minister having represented to him with unusual firmness, that such an unheard of favour conferred upon a foreigner, might alienate the hearts of his own subjects, he countermanded that order, and Candide was carried back to his apartment.

They put him to bed, after having bathed his feet with vinegar. All the grandees came one after another to congratulate him on his good fortune. The Sophi then came to assist him in person, and not only gave him his hand to kiss, according to custom, but likewise struck him a great blow with his fist on the mouth. From whence the politicians conjectured, that Candide would soon make his fortune, and what is very uncommon, though politicians, they were not deceived in the conjecture.

CHAPTER IV

Fresh Favors conferred on Candide ; his great Advancement.

As soon as our hero was cured, he was introduced to the King ; to return him his thanks. The monarch received him in the kindest manner. He gave him two or three hearty boxes on the ear, in the course of their conversation, and conducted him back as far as the guard room, kicking him all the way on the posteriors : at which the courtiers were ready to burst with envy. For since his Majesty had been in a drubbing humour, which was a particular mark of regard, no person had ever been so heartily threshed as Candide.

Three days after this interview, our philosopher, who was almost mad at the favours he had received, and thought that every thing went very bad, was appointed Governor of Chusistan, with an absolute power. He was decorated with a fur cap, which is a grand mark of distinction in Persia. He took his leave of the Sophi, who gave him a few more marks of his kindness, and departed for Sus, the capital of his province. From the moment that Candide made his appearance at court, the grandees had conspired his destruction. The excessive favours which the Sophi had heaped on him, served but to increase the storm ready to burst upon his head. He however thought himself very fortunate, and especially in his removal from court : he enjoyed in prospect the pleasures of high rank, and he said, from the bottom of his heart,

Happy the subjects distant from their prince.

He had not gone quite twenty miles from Ispahan, before five hundred horsemen, armed cap-a-pie, came up with him and his attendants, and discharged a volley of fire-arms upon them. Candide imagined at first that this was intended to do him an honour ; but the ball which broke his leg, soon informed him what was going on. His people laid down their arms, and Candide, more dead than alive, was carried to a castle surrounded by water. His baggage, camels, slaves, white and black eunuchs, with thirty-six women, which the Sophi had given him for his use, all became the prey of the conqueror. Our hero's leg was cut off for fear of a mortification, and care was taken of his life that a more cruel death might be inflicted on him.

O Pangloss ! Pangloss ! what would now become of your Optimism, if you saw me, with only one leg, in the hands of my cruellest enemies ; just as I was entering upon the path of happiness, and was Governor, or King, as one may say, of one of the most considerable provinces of the empire of ancient Media ; when I had camels, slaves, black and white eunuchs, and thirty-six women for my own use, and of which I had not made any use at all ! Thus spoke Candide, as soon as he was able to speak.

But, while he was thus bemoaning himself, every thing was going on for his advantage. The ministry, informed of the outrages committed against him, had detached a body of well disciplined troops in pursuit of the mutineers, and the Monk Ed-Ivan-Baal-Denk, took care to publish, by means of others of his fraternity, that Candide, being the work of the Monks, was consequently the work of God. Such as were in the secret of this attempt were so much the more ready to discover it, as the ministers of religion gave assurance on the part of Mahomet, that every one who had eaten pork, drank wine, omitted bathing for any number of days together ; or had conversed with women at the time of their impurity, against the express prohibitions of the

Alcoran, should be, *ipso facto*, absolved, upon declaring what they knew concerning the conspiracy. They soon discovered the place of Candide's confinement, which they broke open ; and, as it was now become a religious business, the party worsted were exterminated to a man, agreeable to custom in that case. Candide marching over a heap of dead bodies, made his escape, triumphed over the greatest peril he had hitherto encountered, and with his attendants resumed the road to his government. He was received there as a favourite who had been honoured with fifty blows of a bull's pizzle on the soles of his feet, in the presence of the King of Kings.

CHAPTER V

How Candide becomes a very great Man, and yet is not contented.

THE good of philosophy is to make us love each other. Paschal is almost the only philosopher who seems desirous to make us hate our neighbours. Candide had fortunately not read Paschal, and he loved poor human nature very cordially. This was soon perceived by the upright part of the people. They had always kept at a distance from the pretended Ambassadors of heaven, but made no scruple of visiting Candide, and assisting him with their counsels. He made several wise regulations for the encouragement of agriculture, population, commerce, and the arts. He rewarded those who had made useful experiments ; and even encouraged such as had made nothing but books. When the people in my province are in general content, said he, with a charming candour, possibly I shall be so myself. Candide was a stranger to mankind ; he saw himself torn to pieces in seditious libels, and calumniated in a work, intituled, The Friend of Mankind. He found that while he was labouring to make people happy, he had only made them ungrateful. Ah ! cried Candide, what a plague it is to govern these beings without feathers, which vegetate on the earth ! Why am I not still in Propontis, in the company of Master Pangloss, Mistress Cunégonde, the daughter of Pope Urban X. with only one buttock, Brother Giroflée, and the luxurious Pacquette.

CHAPTER VI

The Pleasures of Candide.

CANDIDE, in the bitterness of his grief, wrote a
very pathetic letter to the Rev. Ed-Ivan-Baal-
Denk. He painted to him in such lively colours
the present state of his soul, that Ed-Ivan, greatly
affected with it, obtained the Sophi's consent that
Candide should resign his employments. His
Majesty, in recompense of his services, granted
him a very considerable pension. Eased from
the weight of grandeur, our philosopher immediately sought after Pangloss's Optimism
in the pleasures of a private life. He till then
had lived for the benefit of others, and seemed to
have forgotten that he had a seraglio.

He now called it to remembrance, with that
emotion which the very name inspires. Let every
thing be got ready, says he to his first eunuch,
for my visiting the women. My Lord, answered
the shrill-piped Gentleman, it is now that your
Excellency deserves the title of Wise. The men,
for whom you have done so much, were not
worthy of your attention ; but the women——
That may be, said Candide, modestly.

Embosomed in a garden, where art had assisted
nature to unfold her beauties, stood a small
house, of simple and elegant structure ; and by

that means alone very different from those which are to be seen in the suburbs of the finest city in Europe. Candide blushed as he drew near it: The air round this charming retreat diffused a delicious perfume ; the flowers, amorously intermingled, seemed here to be guided by the instinct of pleasure, and preserved for a long time their various beauties. Here the rose never lost its brilliancy : the view of a rock from which the waters precipitated themselves, with a murmuring and confused noise, invited the soul to that soft melancholy which is ever the forerunner of pleasure. Candide enters, trembling, into a saloon, where taste and magnificence were united : his senses are drawn by a secret charm : he casts his eyes on young Telemachus, who breathes on the canvas, in the midst of the nymphs of Calypso's court. He next turns them to Diana, half naked, who flies into the arms of the tender Endymion ; his agitation increases at the sight of a Venus, faithfully copied from that of Medicis : his ears on a sudden are struck with a divine harmony ; a company of young Circassian females appear covered with their veils ; they form round him a sort of dance, agreeably designed, and much more suitable to the scene than those trifling ballets that are performed on as trifling stages, after the representation of the death of Cæsar and Pompey.

At a signal given they throw off their veils, and discover faces full of expression, that lend new life to the diversion. These beauties studied

the most seducing attitudes, without appearing
to have studied them : one expressed in her
looks a passion without bounds ; another a
soft languor, which waits for pleasures without
seeking them : this fair stoops and raises herself
precipitately, to give a cursory view of those
enchanting charms, which the fair sex display so
freely at Paris ; and that other throws aside a
part of her cymar to show a leg, which alone is
capable of enflaming a mortal of any feeling.
The dance ceases, and they remain fixed, as it
were in the most seducing attitudes.

This pause recalls Candide to himself. The
fire of love takes possession of his breast : he
darts the most ardent looks on all around him ;
imprints warm kisses on lips as warm, and eyes
that swim in liquid fire : he passes his hands over
globes whiter than alabaster, whose elastic motion
repels the touch ; admires their proportion ;
perceives little vermillion protuberances, like
those rose buds which only wait the genial rays
of the sun to unfold them : he kisses them with
rapture, and his lips for some time remained as
if glued to the spot.

Our philosopher next admires, for a while, a
majestic figure, of a fine and delicate shape.
Burning with desire, he at length throws the
handkerchief to a young person, whose eyes he
had observed to be always fixed upon him, and
which seemed to say, Teach me the meaning of a
trouble I am ignorant of ; and who, blushing at
the secret avowal, became a thousand times more

charming. The eunuch, in a moment, opens the
door of a private chamber, consecrated to the
mysteries of love. The lovers enter ; and the
eunuch whispers his master, Here it is, my Lord,
you are going to be truly happy. I hope so, with
all my heart, said Candide.

The ceiling and walls of this little retreat, were
covered with looking-glass : in the midst was
placed a couch of black satin, on which Candide
threw the young Circassian, and undressed her
with incredible haste. The lovely creature let
him do as he pleased, and gave him no other
interruption, but to imprint kisses, full of fire,
on his lips. My Lord, said she to him in the
Turkish language, how fortunate is your slave,
to be thus honoured with your transports ! An
energy of sentiment can be expressed in every
language by those who truly feel it. These few
words enchanted our philosopher : he was no
longer himself ; all he saw, all he heard, was new
to him. What difference between Mistress
Cunégonde, grown ugly, and ravished by Bulgarian freebooters, and a Circassian girl of eighteen, till then an unspotted virgin. This was
the first time of the wise Candide's enjoying her.
The objects which he devoured were reflected
in the glasses ; on what side soever he cast his
eyes, he saw upon the black satin the most beautiful, and fairest form possible, and the contrast
of colours lent it new lustre, with round, firm,
and plump thighs, an admirable fall of loins,
a——but I am obliged to have a regard to the

false delicacy of our language. It is sufficient for me to say, that our philosopher tasted, again and again, that portion of happiness he was capable of receiving ; and that the young Circassian in a little time proved his sufficing reason.

O master ! my dear master Pangloss ! cried Candide, almost beside himself, every thing here is as well as in El Dorado ; a fine woman is alone sufficient to crown the wishes of man. I am as happy as it is possible to be. Leibnitz is in the right, and you are a great philosopher. For instance ; I'll answer for it, that you, my lovely girl, have always had a bias towards Optimism because you have always been happy. Alas ! no ; answered she, I do not know what Optimism is ; but I swear to you, that your slave has not known happiness till to-day. If my Lord is pleased to give me leave, I will convince him of it, by a succinct recital of my adventures. I am very willing, said Candide ; I am now in a pretty calm situation for hearing an historical detail. Upon which the fair slave began her story in the following words:

CHAPTER VII

The History of Zirza.

My father was a Christian, and so likewise am I, as he indeed told me. He had a little hermitage near Cotatis, where, by his fervent devotion, and practising austerities shocking to human nature, he acquired the veneration of the faithful. Crowds of women came to pay him their homage, and took a particular satisfaction in anointing his posteriors, which he lashed every day with several smart strokes of discipline : doubtless it was to one of the most devout of these visitants that I owe my being. I was brought up in a cave, very near to my father's little cell. I was twelve years of age, and had not yet left this tomb, as it may be called, when the earth shook with a dreadful noise ; the arch of the vault fell in, and I was drawn out from under the rubbish half dead, when light struck my eyes for the first time. After such a miraculous escape, my father took me into his hermitage as a Child of Providence. The whole of this adventure appeared wonderful to the people ; my father cried it up as a miracle, and so did they.

I was therefore called Zirza, which in Persian signifies Child of Providence. Notice was soon taken of my little attractions : the women already came but seldom to the hermitage, and the men much oftener. One of them told me that he loved me. Villain, says my father to him, hast thou a fortune sufficient to love her ? This child is a deposit, which God has entrusted to me : he has even appeared to me this night, in the form of a venerable hermit, and forbid me to part with her, for less than a thousand sequins. Retire poor wretch, lest thine impure breath should blast her charms. I have indeed, answered he, only a heart to offer her ; but say, barbarian, dost thou not blush to make a mockery of God, for the gratifying thine avarice ? With what front, vile wretch, darest thou pretend that God has spoken to thee ? This is throwing the greatest contempt upon the Author of Beings, to represent him conversing with such men as thou art. O blasphemy ! cried my father in a rage, God himself has commanded to stone blasphemers. As he spoke these words, he fell upon my lover, and with repeated blows laid him dead on the ground, and his blood flew in my face. Though I had not yet known what love is, this man had interested me, and his death threw me into an affliction so much the greater, as it rendered the sight of my father insupportable to me. I took a resolution to leave him; he somehow perceived my design. Ungrateful, says he to me, it is to me thou owest thy being. Thou art my daughter,—and thou hatest me: but I am going to deserve thy hatred, by the most rigorous treatment. He kept his word but too well with me, cruel man ! During five years, which I spent in tears and groans, neither my youth, nor my beauty, fading through his cruelty, could in the least abate his wrath. Sometimes he stuck a thousand pins into all the parts of my body : at other times, with his discipline, he made the blood trickle down my thighs.—That, says Candide, gave you less pain than the pins. True, my Lord, answers Zirza. At last, continued she, I fled from my paternal habitation ; and, not daring to trust any one, I flung myself into the thickest part of the woods, where I was three days without food, and should have perished with hunger, had it not been for a tyger I was so fortunate as to please, and which was willing to share with me the prey he catched. But I had many horrors to encounter from this formidable beast ; and the brute was very near depriving me of the flower, which you, my Lord, have plucked from me, with so much pain and pleasure. Bad food gave me the scurvy. Scarcely was I cured, before I joined company with a merchant of slaves, who was going to Teflis ; the plague was there then, and I caught it. These various misfortunes did not alter my features, nor hinder the Sophi's purveyor from buying me for your use. I have languished in tears these three months, that I have been among the number of your women. My companions and I imagined ourselves to be the objects of your contempt ; and if you knew, my Lord, how miserable eunuchs are, and how little adapted for comforting young girls who are despised—In short, I am not yet eighteen years of age ; and of these I have spent twelve in a frightful cavern ; I have felt an earthquake ; been covered with the blood of the first lovely man I ever saw ; endured, for the space of four years, the most cruel tortures from my father, and have had the scurvy, and the plague. Consumed with desires, amidst a crew of black and white monsters, still preserving that which I have saved from the fury of an aukward tyger ; and, cursing my fate, I have passed three months in this seraglio ; where I should have died of the jaundice, had not your Excellency honoured me at last with your embraces. O heavens ! cried Candide, is it possible that you have experienced such sensible misfortunes at so tender an age ? What would Pangloss say could he hear your story ? But your misfortunes are at an end, as well as mine. Things do not go badly now ; is not this true ? Upon that Candide resumed his caresses, and was more than ever confirmed in the belief of Pangloss's system.

CHAPTER VIII

Candide's Disgusts. An unexpected Meeting.

Our philosopher, luxuriously settled in the midst of his seraglio, dispensed his favors equally. He sometimes tasted the pleasures of variety, and always returned to the Child of Providence with fresh ardour. But this did not last long ; he soon felt violent pains in his loins, and excruciating cholics. He grew very thin as he grew happy. Zirza's breasts then began to appear not quite so fair, or so well placed ; her thighs not so hard, nor so plump ; her eyes lost all their vivacity in those of Candide ; her complexion, its lustre ; and her lips that beautiful carnation which had enchanted him at first sight. He now perceived that she walked badly, and had a bad smell : he saw, with the greatest disgust, a spot upon the mount of Venus, which he had never observed before to be tainted with any blemish : the affectionate ardour of Zirza became burdensome to him : he was now cool enough to observe the faults of his other women, which had escaped him in his first transports of passion : he saw nothing in them but a shameful wantonness : he was ashamed to have walked in the steps of the wisest of men ; and " he found women more bitter than death."

Candide, always full of these christian sentiments, spent his leisure time in walking over the
streets of Sus ; when one day a cavalier, in a
superb dress, came up and embraced him suddenly, and called him by his name.   Is it possible!
cried Candide, my Lord, that you are—it is not
possible ; otherwise you are so very like—the
Abbé of Perigord—I am the very man, answered
the Abbé.   Upon this Candide started back,
and, with his usual ingenuousness, said, Are you
happy, Master Abbé ?   A fine question, replied
the Abbé ? the little deceit which I put upon you,
contributed not a little to bring me into credit.
The police employed me for some time ; but,
having fallen out with them, I quitted the
ecclesiastical habit, which was no longer of any
advantage to me.   I went over into England,
where persons of my profession drive a better
trade.   I said all I knew, and all I did not know,
about the strength and weakness of the country
I had lately left.   I especially gave bold as-
surances, that the French were the scum of the
earth, and that good sense dwelt no where but in
London.   In short, I made a splendid fortune,
and have just concluded a treaty at the Court of
Persia, which tends to exterminate all the
Europeans, who come for cotton and silk into
the Sophi's dominions, to the prejudice of the
English traders.   The object of your mission is
very commendable, truly, says our Philosopher ;
but, Master Abbé, you are a rogue ; I detest
rogues, and I have some credit at Court.

Tremble ; for now your good fortune has arrived
at its utmost limits ; you are just upon the point
of suffering the fate you deserve. My Lord
Candide, cried the Abbé, throwing himself on
his knees, have pity on me : I feel myself drawn
to evil by an irresistible force, as you find yourself
necessitated to the practice of virtue. This
fatal propensity I have perceived, from the
moment I became acquainted with Mr. Wasp,
and worked at the Feuilles. What do you call
Feuilles? says Candide. Feuilles, answered the
Abbé, are sheets of seventy-two pages in print,
in which the public are entertained with a mixture of calumny, satire, and dullness. An honest
man who can just read and write, and not being
able to continue among the Jesuits so long as he
chose, has set himself to compose this pretty little
work, that he may have wherewithal to buy his
wife lace, and bring up his children in the fear
of God ; and there are also, some other honest
people, who, for a few pence, and some bottles
of bad wine, assist the man in carrying on his
scheme. This Mr. Wasp is, besides, a member
of a very facetious club, who divert themselves
with making poor ignorant people drunk, and
setting them to blaspheme ; or in bullying a
poor simple devil, and breaking his furniture, and
afterwards challenging him. Such little pretty
amusements these gentry call mistifications, and
richly deserve the attention of the police. In
fine, this very honest man, Mr. Wasp, who, if
you will take his word, never was in the gallies,

is troubled with a lethargy, which renders him insensible to the severest home-truths ; and out of which he can be drawn only by certain violent methods, which he submits to, with a resignation and courage above conception. I have worked for some time under this famous writer ; I am become an eminent writer in my turn, and I had but just quitted Mr. Wasp, to set up for myself, when I had the honour of paying you a visit at Paris. You are a very great cheat, Master Abbé, said Candide, yet your sincerity in this point makes some impression upon me. Go to court ; ask for the Rev. Ed-Ivan-Baal-Denk ; I shall write to him in your behalf, but upon express condition, that you promise me to become an honest man ; and that you will not hereafter be the occasion of the murder of thousands, for the sake of a little silk and cotton. The Abbé promised all that Candide required, and they parted very good friends.

CHAPTER IX

Candide's Disgraces, Travels, and Adventures.

THE Abbé Perigourdin was no sooner arrived at court, than he employed all his skill in order to ingratiate himself with the minister, and ruin his benefactor. He spread a report, that Candide was a traitor, and that he had spoke disrespectfully of the sacred whiskers of the King of Kings. All the courtiers condemned him to be burnt in a slow fire ; but the Sophi, more indulgent, only sentenced him to perpetual banishment, after having previously kissed the soles of his accuser's feet, according to the usage among the Persians. The Abbé went in person to put the sentence in execution : he found our philosopher in pretty good health, and disposed to become again happy. My friend, says the English Ambassador to him, I come with regret to let you know, that you must quit this kingdom with all expedition, and kiss my feet, with a true repentance for your enormous guilt. Kiss your feet, Master Abbé ! certainly you are not in earnest, and I do not understand such jokes. Upon which some mutes, who had attended the Abbé, entered, and took off his shoes, acquainting Candide, by signs, that he must submit to this piece of humiliation, or else expect to be impaled. Candide, by virtue of his free will, kissed the Abbé's feet. They put on him a coarse linen robe, and the executioner drove him out of the town, crying all the time, Behold the traitor ! who has spoken irreverently of the Sophi's whiskers ! irreverently of the Imperial whiskers !

What did the officious monk, while his favourite, whom he protected, was treated thus ? I know nothing of that. It is probable that he was tired of protecting Candide. Who can depend on the favour of Kings, still less on that of monks?

In the mean time our hero went melancholy on. I never even mentioned, said he to himself, the King of Persia's whiskers. I am fallen in an instant from the pinnacle of happiness into the abyss of misery; because a wretch, who has violated all laws, accuses me of a pretended crime which I have never committed; and this wretch, this monster, this persecutor of virtue—he is happy.

Candide, after travelling on foot for some days, found himself upon the frontiers of Turkey. He directed his course towards the Propontis, with a design to settle there again, and pass the rest of his days in the cultivation of his garden. He saw, as he entered a little village, a great croud of people, all in an uproar: he inquired into the cause of it. Something rather singular, says an old man to him. It is some time ago since the wealthy Mahomet demanded in marriage the daughter of the Janissary Zamoud: he found her not to be a virgin; and in pursuance of a principle quite natural, and authorised by the laws, he sent her home to her father, after having disfigured her face. Zamoud, exasperated at the disgrace brought on his family, in the first transports of a fury equally natural, with one stroke of his scymetar clove the disfigured visage of his daughter. His eldest son, who loved his sister passionately, which is likewise very natural, flew upon his father, and naturally too, plunged a very sharp poniard into his breast. Afterwards, like a lion who grows more enraged at seeing his own blood flow, the furious Zamoud ran to Mahomet's house ; and after striking to the ground some slaves, who opposed his passage, murdered Mahomet, his wives, and two children then in the cradle ; all which was very natural, considering the violent ferment he then was in. At last, to crown all, he killed himself with the same poniard, reeking with the blood of his father and his enemies, which is also very natural, What a scene of horrors ! cried Candide. What would you have said, master Pangloss, had you found such barbarities in nature ? Would not you acknowledge that nature is corrupted, that all is not——No, says the old man, for the pre-established harmony——O' heavens! do ye not deceive me ? Is this Pangloss, says Candide, whom I again see ? The very same, answered the old man : I recollected you, but I was willing to find out your sentiments, before I would discover myself. Come, let us discourse a little on contingent effects, and see if you have made any progress in the art of wisdom. Alas ! says Candide, you chuse your time very ill for such a discussion ; rather let me know what is become of Mistress Cunégonde ; tell me where are brother Giroflée, Pacquette, and Pope Urban's daughter. I know nothing of them, says Pangloss ; it is now two years since I left our habitation in order to find you out. I have travelled over almost all Turkey : I was upon the point of setting out for the Court of Persia, where I heard you made a great figure, and I only tarried in this little village, among these good people, till I had gathered strength for continuing my journey. What is this I see ? answered Candide, quite surprised. You want an arm, my dear Doctor. That is nothing, says the one-armed and the one-eyed doctor : nothing is more common in the best of worlds, than to see persons who want one eye and one arm. I met with this misfortune in a journey from Mecca. Our caravan was attacked by a troop of Arabs : our guard attempted to make resistance ; and, according to the rules of war, the Arabs, who found themselves to be the strongest, massacred us all without mercy. There perished about five hundred persons in this attack, among whom was about a dozen big-bellied women. For my part, I had only my skull split, and an arm cut off ; I did not die of my wounds, and I still found that every thing happened for the best. But as to yourself, my dear Candide, whence is it that you have a wooden leg ? Upon this Candide began, and gave an account of his adventures. Our philosophers turned together towards the Propontis, and enlivened their journey by discoursing on physical and moral evil, free-will and predestination, monads and pre-established harmony.

CHAPTER X

*Candide and Pangloss arrive in the Propontis ;
what they saw there ; and what became of
them.*

O CANDIDE ! said Pangloss, what made you
grow tired of cultivating your garden ? Why
did we not still continue to eat citrons and
pistachio nuts ? Why was you weary of being
happy ? Certainly, because every thing is necessary in the best of worlds, there was a necessity
that you should undergo the bastinado, in the
presence of the King of Persia ; have your leg
cut off, in order to make Chusistan happy, to
experience the ingratitude of mankind, and draw
down upon the heads of some atrocious villains
the punishment which they had deserved. With
such conversation, they arrived at their old
dwelling. The first objects that presented themselves were Martin and Pacquette, in the habit
of slaves. Whence, said Candide to them, is
this metamorphosis ? after having tenderly embraced them. Alas ! answered they sobbing,
You have no longer any house of your own ;
another has undertaken the cultivating your
garden ; he eats your preserved citrons and
pistachios, and treats us like negroes. Who,
says Candide, is this other ? The High Admiral,

answered they, a human being, the least humane
of all human beings. The Sultan, willing to
recompence his services without putting himself
to any expence, has confiscated all your goods,
under pretext that you had gone over to his
enemies, and has condemned us to slavery. Be
advised by me, Candide, added Martin, never
stop here, but continue your journey. I always
told you every thing is for the worst ; the sum
of evil exceeds by much that of good. Be gone,
and I do not despair but you may become a
Manichean, if you are not already. Pangloss was
very desirous of beginning an argument in form,
in favour of Optimism ; but Candide interrupted
him, to ask about Mistress Cunégonde, the old
woman, brother Giroflée, and Cacambo. Cacambo, answered Martin, is here ; he is at
present employed about emptying a house of
office. The old woman is dead of a kick in the
stomach, given her by an eunuch. Brother
Giroflée has entered among the janissaries.
Mistress Cunégonde has recovered her plump-
ness, and former beauty ; she is in our master's
seraglio. What a chain of misfortunes, says
Candide ! Was there a necessity for Mistress
Cunégonde to become handsome, only to make
me a cuckold ? It is of little consequence, says
Pangloss, whether Mistress Cunégonde be beautiful or ugly, or that she be in your arms or those
of another, all this is nothing to the general
system : for my part I wish her a numerous
posterity. Philosophers do not perplex them-

selves by whom women have children, provided they have them. Population—Alas! says Martin, philosophers ought much rather to employ themselves in rendering a few individuals happy, than engaging them to multiply the number of sufferers. While they were thus arguing, a great noise was heard on a sudden ; it was the Admiral diverting himself, by causing a dozen slaves to be whipped. Pangloss and Candide, terrified to death, with tears in their eyes parted from their friends, and in all haſte took the road to Conſtantinople.

There they found all the people in a great ſtir. A fire had broke out in the suburb of Pera ; five or six hundred houses were already consumed, and two or three thousand persons perished in the flames. What a horrible disaſter ! cried Candide. All is for the beſt ; says Pangloss ; these little accidents happen every year. It is very natural for the fire to catch houses built of wood, and for those who are in them to be burnt ; besides, this procures some relief to many honeſt people, who languish in poverty and misery.— What is this I hear ? says an officer of the Sublime Porte : How, wretch, dareſt thou say that all is for the beſt, when half Conſtantinople is in flames ? Dog, be thou cursed of our Prophet ; Go, receive the punishment due to thy impudence! And as he uttered these words he took Pangloss by the middle, and flung him headlong into the flames. Candide, half dead with fright, and scarce able to ſtand, made his way, as well as he could, to a neighbouring quarter, where all was more quiet ; and we shall see what became of him in the next chapter.

CHAPTER XI

Candide continues his Travels, and in what Quality.

I HAVE now no other choice to make, said Candide, but to become a slave, or turn Turk. Happiness has abandoned me for ever. A turban would corrupt all my pleasures. My mind would never be at ease, in a religion full of imposture, and into which I had entered merely from a motive of vile interest. No, I shall never be at rest, if I cease to be an honest man : let me make myself then a slave. Candide had no sooner taken this resolution than he set about putting it into execution. He chose an Armenian Merchant for his Master, who was a man of very good character, and passed for virtuous, as much as an Armenian can be. He gave Candide two hundred sequins, as the price of his liberty. The Armenian was just setting out for Norway ; he took Candide with him, in hopes that a philosopher would be of use to him in his traffic. They embarked, and the wind was so favourable, that they were not above half the usual time in their passage. They even had no occasion to purchase a favourable gale from the Lapland witches, and contented themselves with giving them some ſtock-fish, that they might not spoil their good fortune with their enchantments ; which sometimes happens, if we may believe Moreri's Dictionary on this head.

The Armenian no sooner landed than he provided a ſtock of whale-blubber, and ordered our philosopher to go over all the country to buy him some dried salt fish: he acquitted himself of his commission in the beſt manner he could, returned with several rein-deers loaded with this merchandise, and made many sagacious reflections on the aſtonishing difference which is to be found between the Laplanders and other men. A very diminutive female Laplander, whose head was a little bigger than her body, her eyes red and full of fire, a flat nose, and mouth as wide as possible, bid him good morrow, with admirable grace. My little Lord, says this being, (a foot and ten inches high) to him, I think you very handsome ; do me the favour to love me a little. So saying, she flew to him and caught him round the neck. Candide pushed her away with horror. She immediately cries out, when in comes her husband with several other Laplanders. What is the occasion of all this uproar ? say they. It is, answers the little thing, that this ſtranger—Alas ! I am choaked with grief; he despises me. Oh! I underſtand you, says the Lapland husband, thou unpolite, dishonest, brutal, infamous, cowardly rascal ; thou hast disgraced my whole family ; thou dost me the most sensible injury ; thou refusest to lie with my wife. Why here's a fellow for you, cried our hero : What would you have said then, if I had lain with her ? I would have wished thee all earthly happiness ; says the Laplander to him in a rage, but thou only deservest my indignation. At these words, he discharged on Candide's back a volley of blows with a cudgel. The rein-deer were seized by the relations of the offended husband, and Candide, for fear of worse, was forced to betake himself to flight, and renounce his good master for ever : for how would he venture to present himself before him without money, whale-blubber, or rein-deer?

CHAPTER XII

Candide still continues his Travels. New Adventures.

CANDIDE travelled a long time without determining whither he should go, at length he resolved to go to Denmark, where he had heard that every thing went on pretty well. He had a few pieces of money about him, which the Armenian had made him a present of ; and with this slender support he should get to the end of his journey. Hope rendered his misery supportable to him, and he still passed at times some happy moments. He found himself one day in an inn with three travellers, who talked to him with great warmth about a *plenum* and the *materia subtilis*. Mighty well, says Candide to himself, these are philosophers. Gentlemen, says he to them, a *plenum* is incontestible ; there is no *vacuum* in nature, and the *materia subtilis* is a well-imagined hypothesis. You are then a Cartesian ? says the three travellers. Yes, answers Candide, and a Leibnitizian, which is more. So much the worse for you, replied the philosophers. Des Cartes and Leibnitz had not common sense. We are Newtonians, and we glory in it ; if we dispute, it is only the better to confirm ourselves in our opinions, for we all think alike. We search for truth in Newton's tract, because we are persuaded that Newton is a great man—And Des Cartes too, and Leibnitz and Pangloss likewise, says Candide: these great men are worth a thousand of yours. You are a fool, friend, answered the philosophers : do you know the laws of refraction, attraction, and motion ? Have you read the truths which Dr. Clarke has published, in answer to the reveries of your Leibnitz ? Do you know what centrifugal and centripetal force is ? and that colours depend on their density ? Have you any notion of the theory of light and gravitation ?

Do you know the period of twenty-five thousand nine hundred and twenty years, which unluckily do not agree with chronology ? No, undoubtedly, you have but false ideas of all these things : peace, then, thou contemptible monad, and beware how you insult giants by comparing them to pygmies. Gentlemen, answered Candide, were Pangloss here, he would tell you very fine things ; for he is a great philosopher : he has a sovereign contempt for your Newton ; and, as I am his disciple, I likewise set no great store by him. The philosophers, enraged beyond measure, fell upon poor Candide, and drubbed him most philosophically.

Their wrath subsiding, they asked our hero's pardon for their too great warmth. Upon this, one of them began a very fine harangue on mildness, moderation, and command of the passions.

While they were talking, they saw a magnificent funeral pass by ; our philosophers from thence took occasion to descant on the foolish vanity of man. Would it not be more reasonable, says one of them, that the relations and friends of the deceased should, without pomp and noise, carry the bier themselves ? Would not this funeral act, by offering to their minds a strong idea of death, produce an effect the most salutary, the most philosophical ? This reflection, for instance, which would offer itself, " The body I " carry is that of my friend, my relation; he is no " more ; and, like him, I must cease to be in this " world " : would not this, I say, be a means of lessening the number of crimes in this vile world, and of bringing back to virtue, beings who believe the immortality of the soul ? Men are too apt to smother the thoughts of death, for fear of presenting too ſtrong images of it to their minds. Whence is it that people remove from such diſtressing sights, as a mother and a wife in tears ? The plaintive accents of nature, the piercing cries of despair, would do much greater honour to the ashes of the dead, than all these individuals clad in black from head to foot, together with useless female mourners, and that crowd of miniſters, who chaunt their funeral orations so pleasantly, which the deceased do not hear.

This is extremely well spoken, says Candide ; and did you always talk as well without thinking proper to thresh people, you would be great philosophers.

Our travellers parted with expressions of mutual confidence and friendship. Candide ſtill continued travelling towards Denmark. He ſtruck into the woods ; where musing deeply on all the misfortunes which had happened to him in this beſt of worlds, he insensibly got out of his road and loſt himself. The day began to close, when he perceived his miſtake : he was seized with dismay, and raising in a melancholy manner his eyes to Heaven, and leaning againſt the trunk of a tree, our hero spoke in the following terms : I have travelled over half the globe ; seen deceit and slander triumphant ; I have only sought to do service to mankind, and I have been persecuted. A great king honours me with his favour and fifty blows of a bull's pizzle. I arrive with a wooden leg in a very fine province ; there I taſte a few pleasures, after having drank deep of affliction. An abbé comes ; I protect him ; he insinuates himself at court through my intereſt, and I am obliged to kiss his feet——I meet with my poor Pangloss only to see him burnt. I find myself in company with philosophers, the mildeſt and moſt sociable of all the species of animals that are spread over the face of the earth, and they beat me unmercifully—— All muſt necessarily be for the beſt, since Pangloss has said it ; but, I am the moſt wretched of all possible beings for all that. Here Candide ſtopt short to liſten to cries of diſtress, which seemed to come from a place near him. He ſtepped forward out of curiosity, when he beheld a young woman tearing her hair with all the signs of the deepeſt anguish. Whoever you are, says she to him, if you have any feeling, follow me. He went with her, but they had not gone many paces before Candide perceived a man and woman ſtretched out on the grass : their faces bespoke the greatness of their souls and nobleness of their birth ; their features though diſtorted by pain, had something so intereſting, that Candide could not forbear bemoaning them, and informing himself, with the utmoſt eagerness, in regard to the cause which reduced them to so miserable a situation. It is my father and mother whom you see, says the young woman : yes, these are the authors of my wretched being, continued she, throwing herself into their arms. They fled to avoid the rigour of an unjust sentence : I accompanied them in their flight, too happy to share in their misfortune, with the sweet hope that in the deserts where we were going to hide ourselves, my feeble hands might procure them a necessary subsistence. We stopped here to take some rest ; I discovered that tree which you see, whose fruit has deceived me—Alas ! Sir, I am a wretch to be viewed with horror by the world and myself ! Arm your hand to avenge offended virtue, and to punish the parricide !—Strike !—this fruit—I presented it to my father and mother ; they ate of it with pleasure : I rejoiced to have found the means of quenching the thirst with which they were tormented.—Unhappy wretch ! it was death I presented to them—this fruit is poison.

This recital made Candide shudder ; his hair stood on end, and a cold sweat bedewed his body. He was eager, as much as his present condition could permit, to give some relief to this unfortunate family; but the poison had already made too much progress ; and the most efficacious remedies would not have been able to stop its fatal effect.

Dear child, our only hope, cried the two unhappy parents, Forgive yourself, as we pardon thee ; it was the excess of thy tenderness which has robbed us of our lives.—Generous stranger, vouchsafe to take care of her ; her heart is noble and formed to virtue ; she is a deposit which we leave in your hands, infinitely more precious to us, than all our paſt fortune—Dear Zenoida, receive our laſt embraces ; mingle thy tears with ours. Heavens ! how happy are these moments to us ! Thou haſt opened to us the dreary cave in which we languished for forty years paſt. Tender Zenoida, we bless thee ; mayſt thou never forget the lessons which our experience hath dictated to thee ; and may they preserve thee from the abyss of misery, which seems already open at thy feet.

They expired as they pronounced these words. Candide had great difficulty to bring Zenoida to herself. The moon had enlightened the affecting scene ; the day now appeared, and Zenoida, plunged in sad affliction, had not as yet recovered the use of her senses. As soon as she opened her eyes, she entreated Candide to endeavour to open the earth, in order to inter the bodies : she assiſted in the work with an aſtonishing courage. This duty fulfilled, she gave free scope to her tears. Our philosopher drew her away from this fatal place : they travelled a long time without observing any certain route. At length, they perceived a little cottage ; two persons in the decline of life dwelt in this desert, who were always ready to give every assiſtance in their power, to their fellow-creatures in diſtress. These old people were such as Philemon and Baucis are described to us. For fifty years they had taſted the soft endearments of marriage, without ever experiencing its bitterness ; an unimpaired health, the fruit of temperance and tranquillity of mind, mild and simple manners ; a fund of inexhauſtible candour in their character ; all the virtues which man owes to himself, formed the glorious, and only fortune which Heaven had beſtowed upon them. They were held in veneration in the neighbouring villages, whose inhabitants, happy in an innocent ruſticity, might have passed for very good sort of people had they been catholics. These villagers looked upon it as a duty not to suffer Agaton and Sunama (for so the old couple were called) to want for any thing, and their charity extended to the new comers. Alas ! said Candide, it is a great pity my dear Pangloss, that you were burnt : you had certainly some reason on your side ; but yet it is not in all the parts of Europe and Asia, which I have travelled over in your company, that every thing is for the beſt : it is only in El Dorado, whither no one can go ; and in a little cottage, situated in the coldeſt, moſt barren, and frightful region in the world. What pleasure should I have to hear you discourse about the pre-eſtablished harmony and monads ? I should be very willing to pass my days among these honeſt Lutherans ; but then I muſt give up going to mass, and submit to be torn to pieces in the CHRETIEN.

Candide was very inquisitive to learn the adventures of Zenoida, but discretion and politeness withheld him from speaking to her about it ; she perceived his delicacy, and satisfied his impatience in the following terms.

CHAPTER XIII

The History of Zenoida. How Candide fell in love with her; and what followed.

I AM descended from one of the most ancient families in Denmark ; one of my ancestors perished at that horrid feast which the wicked Christiern prepared for the destruction of so many senators. The riches and honours which have been heaped upon our family, have hitherto served only to make them more eminently unfortunate. My father had the resolution to displease a great man in power, by boldly telling him the truth : he was presently accused by suborned witnesses of a number of crimes which had no foundation. His judges were deceived by false evidence. Alas ! where is that judge who can always discover those snares which envy and treachery lay for unguarded innocence ! My father was sentenced to the scaffold. He had no way left to avoid his fate but by flight: accordingly he withdrew to the house of an old friend, whom he thought deserving of that glorious title : we remained some time concealed in a castle belonging to him on the sea-side ; and we might have continued there to this day, had not the base wretch taking advantage of our being in his power, attempted to repay himself for the services he did us, at a price that gave us all reason to detest him. This infamous monster had conceived a most unnatural passion for my mother and myself at the same time ; he attempted our virtue by methods the most unworthy of a man of honour ; and we were reduced to the necessity of exposing ourselves to the most dreadful dangers to avoid the effects of his brutal passion. In a word, we took to flight a second time, and you know the melancholy sequel.

At the close of this short narrative, Zenoida burst into tears afresh. Candide wiped them from her eyes, and said to her, by way of consolation, " Madam, every thing is for the best ; " if your father had not died by poison, he would " infallibly have been discovered, and then his " head would have been cut off. The good " lady, your mother, would, in all probability " have died of grief, and we should not have been " in this poor hut, where every thing is a great " deal better than the finest of all possible castles." Alas ! Sir, replied Zenoida, my father never told me that every thing was for the best ; we are all children of the same divine Father, who loves us, but who has not exempted us from the most calamitous sorrows, the most grievous maladies, and an innumerable tribe of miseries that afflict the human race. Poison grows by the side of the salutiferous quinquina, in America. The happiest of all mortals has some time or other shed tears. What we call life, is a compound of pleasure and pain ; it is the lapse of a certain stated portion of time which always appears too long in the sight of the wise man, and which every one ought to employ in doing good to the community in which he is placed ; in the enjoyment of the works of Providence, without idly seeking after their hidden causes ; in regulating our conduct by the rules of conscience ; and, above all, in showing a due respect to religion. Too happy when we can live up to it.

These things my ever-respected father has frequently inculcated to me. Unhappy are those rash and inconsiderate writers, he would often say, who attempt to pry into the hidden ways of Providence. From the principle, that God will be honoured from thousands of atoms, mankind have blended the most absurd chimeras with respectable truths. The Turkish Dervise, the Persian Bramin, the Chinese Bonza, and the Indian Talapoin, all worship the Deity in a different manner: but they enjoy a tranquillity of soul amidst the darkness in which they are plunged ; and he who would endeavour to enlighten them, does them but ill service. It is doing no kindness to mankind to tear the bandage of prejudice from their eyes.

You talk like a philosopher, said Candide ; may I ask you, my fair lady, of what religion you are ? I was brought up in the Lutheran profession, answered Zenoida. I must confess, says Candide, that every word you have spoke, has been like a ray of light that has penetrated my very soul, and I find a sort of esteem and admiration for you, that—But how, in the name of wonder, came so bright an understanding to be lodged in so beautiful a form ? Upon my word, Mistress, I esteem and admire you, as I said before, so much that—Candide stammered out a few words more, when Zenoida, perceiving his confusion, quitted him, and from that moment carefully avoided all occasions of being alone with him ; and Candide, on his part, sought every opportunity of being alone with her, or else being by himself. He was buried in a melancholy that to him had charms ; he was deeply enamoured of Zenoida ; but endeavoured to conceal his passion from himself : his looks, however, too plainly evinced the feelings of his heart. Alas ! would he often say to himself, if Master Pangloss was here, he would give me good advice, for he was a great philosopher.

CHAPTER XIV

Continuation of the Loves of Candide.

THE only consolation that Candide enjoyed, was conversing with Zenoida in the presence of their hosts. How was it possible, said he to her one day, that the Monarch to whom you had access, could suffer such injustice to be done to your family ? Certainly you have sufficient reason to hate him. How ! said Zenoida, who can hate their King ; who can do otherwise than love that person to whose hand is consigned the keen-edged sword of the laws ? Kings are the living images of the Deity, and we ought never to arraign their conduct ; obedience and respect is the duty of a subject. I admire you more and more, said Candide : pray, do you know the great Leibnitz, and the great Pangloss, who was burnt, after having escaped hanging ? Are you acquainted with the monads, the *materia subtilis*, and the vortices ? No, Sir ; replied Zenoida ; I never heard my father mention any of these ; he only gave me a slight tincture of experimental philosophy, and taught me to hold in contempt all those kinds of philosophy that do not directly tend to make mankind happy ; that give him false notions of his duty to himself and his neighbour ; that do not teach him to regulate his

conduct, and fill his mind only with technical
terms, or hazardous conjectures ; that do not
give him a clearer idea of the author of nature than
what he may acquire from his works, and the
wonders that are every day working before our
sight. Still more Madam, do I admire you ;
you enchant me ; you ravish me ; you are an
angel that heaven has sent to remove, from before
my eyes, the mist of Master Pangloss's sophistical
arguments. What a silly animal I was ! after
having been so heartily kicked, flogged, and
bastinadoed on the soles of my feet ; after having
felt the horrors of an earthquake ; having seen
Doctor Pangloss once hanged, and very lately
burnt ; after having been ravished by a villainous
Persian, who put me to the most excruciating
tortures ; after having been robbed by a decree of
the divan, and soundly thrashed by a set of
philosophers : after all these things, I say, to
think that every thing was for the best ! but
now, thank heaven ! I am undeceived. But,
nevertheless, it is certain, nature never appeared
half so charming to me as since I have been
blessed with the sight of you. The rural concert
of the birds charms my ears with an harmony,
to which they were till now utter strangers ; I
breathe a new soul, and the glow of sentiment that
enchants me seems imprinted on every object :
I do not feel that effeminate languor which I did
in the gardens of Sus ; the sensation with which
you inspire me is wholly different. Let us stop
here, said Zenoida ; you seem to be running to

lengths that may, perhaps, offend my delicacy, which you ought to respect. I will be silent then, said Candide ; but my passion will only be the more violent. On saying these words, he looked stedfastly at Zenoida ; he perceived her to blush, and like a man who had profited by experience, he conceived the most flattering hopes from these appearances.

The beautiful Dane still continued for some time to avoid the pursuits of Candide. One day, as he was walking hastily to and fro in the garden, he cried out in a transport of love and tenderness, Ah ! why have I not now my El Dorado sheep ? why have I it not in my power to purchase a small kingdom ? Ah ! was I but a King——What should I be to you ? said a voice, which pierced the heart of our philosopher. Is it you, lovely Zenoida ? cried he, falling on his knees. I thought myself alone. The few words I heard you just now utter seem to promise me the felicity to which my soul aspires. I shall, in all probability, never be a King, nor ever possessed of a fortune ; but, if you love me—Do not turn from me those lovely eyes, but suffer me to read in them a confession, which is alone capable of making me happy. Beauteous Zenoida, I adore you ! Let your heart be open to compassion— What do I see ? you weep ! Ah ! my happiness is too great. Yes, you are happy, said Zenoida ; nothing can oblige me to disguise the feelings of my heart for a person I think deserving of my affection : hitherto you have been attached to my destiny only by the bands of humanity ; it is now time to strengthen those by ties more sacred ; I have consulted my heart, reflect maturely in your turn ; but remember, that if you marry me, you become obliged to be my protector ; to share with me those misfortunes that fate may still, perhaps, have in store for me, and to sooth my sorrows. Marry you ! said Candide ; those words have opened my eyes to the imprudence of my conduct. Alas ! dear Idol of my soul, I am not deserving of your goodness. Cunégonde is still living—Cunégonde ! who is that ? She is my wife, answered Candide, with his usual frankness.

Our two lovers remained some moments without uttering a word ; they tried to speak, but the accents died away on their lips ; their eyes were filled with tears. Candide held the fair Zenoida's hands in his ; he prest them to his heart, and devoured them with kisses : he had even the boldness to raise his hands to the bosom of his mistress ; he found her breath grow short ; his soul flew to his lips, and fixing his mouth to that of Zenoida, he brought the fair one back to those senses which she had nearly lost. Candide thought he read his pardon in her eyes. Dearest lover, said she to him, my anger would but ill repay these transports which my heart approves. Yet hold, you will ruin me in the opinion of the world ; and you yourself would soon cease to love me, when once I was become the object of contempt. Forbear, therefore, and spare my weakness. How ! cried Candide ; because the slaves of prejudice say, that a woman loses her honour by bestowing happiness on a being whom she loves, by following that tender bent of nature, which in the first happy ages of the world—But I will forbear to relate the whole of this interesting conversation, and content myself with saying that the eloquence of Candide, heightened by the warmth of amorous expression, had all the effect that may be imagined on a young tender female philosopher.

The lovers, whose days till then, had slowly crept on in sadness and melancholy, now passed them in a rapid intoxication of amorous joys. Pleasure flowed through their veins in an un-interrupted current. The gloomy woods, the barren mountains, surrounded by horrid pre-cipices, the icy plains, and dreary fields, covered with snow on all sides, convinced them more and more of the necessity of loving each other with ardor. In short, they determined never to quit that dreadful solitude, but fate was not yet weary of persecuting them, as we shall see in the next chapter.

CHAPTER XV

The Arrival of Wolhall.   A Journey to Copenhagen.

THE happy hours of Candide and Zenoida, were
diversified in discoursing on the works of the
Deity, the worship which mankind ought to pay
him, and the mutual duties they owe to each
other, especially that of benevolence, the most
useful of all virtues.   But, they did not confine
themselves to frivolous declamations.   Candide
taught the young men the respect due to the
sacred restraint of the laws ; Zenoida instructed
the young women in the duties they owed their
parents : both joined their endeavours to sow
the hopeful seeds of religion in their young
hearts.   One day, as they were busied in those
pious offices, Sunama came to tell Zenoida, that
an old gentleman, with several servants, was just
alighted at their house ;   and that, by the
description he had given her of a person he was
looking for, she was certain it could be no other
than Zenoida herself.   This stranger had followed Sunama close at her heels, and entered,
almost at the same instant, into the room where
were Candide and Zenoida.

At sight of him Zenoida instantly fainted
away ; but Wolhall, not in the least touched with
her situation, took hold of her hand, and pulled

her to him with so much violence, that it brought her to her senses ; which she had no sooner recovered, than she burst into a flood of tears. So, niece, said he, with a sarcastic smile, I find you in very good company. I do not wonder you prefer them to living in the capital, to my house, and the company of your family. Yes, Sir, replied Zenoida, I do prefer the dwelling of simplicity and truth, to the mansions of treason and imposture. I can never behold but with horror that place where first began my misfortunes ; where I have had so many proofs of the wickedness of your heart, and where I have no other relations but yourself. Come, Madam, said Wolhall, follow me, if you please ; for so you shall, even if you should faint again. Saying this, he dragged her to the door of the house, and made her get into the carriage, which was waiting for him. She had only time to tell Candide to follow, and went away blessing her hosts, and promising to reward them amply for their generous cares.

A domestic of Wolhall pitied the despair in which he saw Candide plunged ; he imagined that he felt no other concern for the fair Dane than what unfortunate virtue inspires : he proposed to him taking a journey to Copenhagen, and he furnished him with the means to accomplish it. He did more ; he insinuated to him that he might be admitted as one of Wolhall's domestics, if he had no other resource than going to service. Candide liked his proposal ; and no sooner arrived than his future fellow-servant presented him as one of his relations, for whom he would be answerable. Rascal, says Wolhall to him, I consent to grant you the honour of serving a person of such rank as I am : but be sure, never forget the profound respect which you owe to my commands ; you must even prevent them, if you have sense enough to do it : I would have you constantly reflect, that a man like me degrades himself in speaking to a wretch such as you. Our philosopher answered with great humility to this impertinent discourse ; and from that day he was clad in his master's livery.

It is easy to imagine the joy and surprise that Zenoida felt when she recognized her lover among her uncle's servants : she contrived various opportunities, which Candide knew how to avail himself of : they swore eternal constancy. Zenoida had some unhappy moments ; she sometimes reproached herself on account of her love for Candide ; she sometimes afflicted him by a few caprices : but Candide idolized her ; he knew that perfection is not the portion of man, and still less so of woman. Zenoida recovered her peace of mind in the arms of her lover. The kind of constraint under which they lay, rendered their pleasures the more exquisite : they were still happy.

CHAPTER XVI

How Candide found his Wife again, and lost his Mistress.

THE haughty treatment of Wolhall was the only hardship our hero had to bear, and that was not purchasing his mistress's favours at too dear a rate. But, successful love is not so easily concealed as many imagine. Our lovers betrayed themselves. Their connection was no longer a secret to any in the house, but the short-sighted eyes of Wolhall ; all the domestics knew it. Candide received congratulations on that head which made him tremble ; he expected the storm, ready to burst upon his head, and did not doubt but a person, who had been dear to him, was upon the point of accelerating his misfortune. He had for some days perceived a face resembling Mistress Cunégonde ; he again saw the same face in Wolhall's court-yard ; but the object which struck him was very meanly drest, and there was no likelihood that a favourite of a great Mahometan should be found in the court-yard of a house at Copenhagen. This disagreeable object, however, looked at Candide very attentively : and coming suddenly up to him, and seizing him by the hair, she gave him the severest blow on the face, that he had ever received in his

life. I am not deceived, cried our Philosopher. O
heavens ! who would have thought it ! What
do you here, after having suffered yourself to be
violated by a follower of Mahomet ? Go, faith-
less spouse, I know you not. Thou shalt know
me, replied Cunégonde, by my fury : I know
the life thou leadest, thy love for thy master's
niece, and thy contempt for me. Alas ! it is
now three months since I quitted the seraglio,
because I was no longer of any use in that place.
A merchant has bought me to mend his linen, he
takes me along with him, when he makes a
voyage to this country ; Martin, Cacambo, and
Pacquette, whom he has also bought, are with
me ; Dr. Pangloss, through the greatest chance
in the world, was in the same vessel as a passenger;
we were shipwrecked some miles from hence ; I
escaped the danger with the faithful Cacambo,
who, I swear to thee, has a skin as fine as thy
own : I behold thee again, and find thee false.
Tremble then, and fear every thing from a pro-
voked wife.

Candide was quite stupefied at this affecting
scene ; he had suffered Cunégonde to part from
him, without reflecting, that proper measures are
always to be kept with those who know our
secrets, when Cacambo presented himself to his
sight : they embraced each other with sincere
regard. Candide informed him of the conversation he had just had with his wife ; he was
very much afflicted for the loss of the great
Pangloss, who, after having been hanged and

burnt, was at laſt unhappily drowned. They spoke with that free effusion of heart which friendſhip alone inspires. A little billet thrown out of the window by Zenoida put an end to the conversation. Candide opened it, and found in it these words:

"Fly, my dear Lover ; all is discovered. An "innocent propensity, which nature authorises, "and does no injury to society, is a crime in the "eyes of credulous and cruel men. Wolhall "has juſt left my chamber, and has treated me "with the utmoſt inhumanity : he is gone to "obtain an order to throw you into prison, "there to perish. Fly, my ever-dear Lover ; "preserve a life which thou canſt not pass any "longer near me. Those happy hours are no "more, in which we gave proofs of our reciprocal "tenderness.—Ah ! wretched Zenoida, how haſt "thou offended heaven, to merit so rigorous a "fate ! But I wander : remember always thy "tender, faithful, Zenoida, and thou, my dear "Lover, shalt live eternally within my heart— "Alas ! thou haſt never known how much I "loved thee——O, that thou couldſt receive "upon my burning lips my laſt adieu, and catch "my laſt sigh ! I find myself ready to join my "unhappy father in the grave ; the light is "hateful to me ; it serves only to discover fresh "cruelties."

Cacambo, always discreet and prudent, drew Candide, who no longer was himself, away with him ; they went the shorteſt way out of the city.

Candide opened not his mouth, and they were already a good way from Copenhagen before he was roused out of that lethargy in which he was buried. At laſt, he looked at his faithful Cacambo, and spoke in these terms.

CHAPTER XVII

How Candide had a Mind to kill himself, and did not do it. What happened to him at an Inn.

DEAR Cacambo, formerly my valet, now my equal, and always my friend, thou haſt had a share in some of my misfortunes ; thou haſt given me salutary advice, and thou haſt been witness to my love for Miſtress Cunégonde. Alas ! my old Maſter, says Cacambo, it is she who has played you this villainous trick ; it is she who, after having learned from your fellow-servants that your love for Zenoida was as great as hers for you, revealed the whole to the barbarous Wolhall. If this is so, says Candide, I have nothing further to do but die. Our philosopher pulled out of his pocket a little knife, and began whetting it with a coolness worthy of an ancient Roman or an Englishman. What are you going to do ? says Cacambo. To cut my throat, answers Candide. An excellent thought ! replied Cacambo ;

Q   219

but the philosopher never resolves but upon reflection : you will always have it in your power to kill yourself, if your mind does not alter. Be advised by me, my dear Master ; defer your resolution till to-morrow ; the longer you delay it, the more courageous will the action be. I approve of thy reasoning, says Candide : besides, if I should cut my throat immediately, the Gazetteer of Trevoux would insult my memory : I am determined, therefore, that I will not kill myself till two or three days hence. As they conversed, they arrived at Elsineur, a pretty considerable town, not far from Copenhagen ; there they lay that night, and Cacambo was delighted to perceive, next morning, the good effect which sleep had produced upon Candide. They left the town at day-break. Candide, still the Philosopher, (for the prejudices of childhood are never effaced) entertained his friend Cacambo on the subject of physical good and evil, the discourses of the sage Zenoida, and the striking truths which he had imbibed from her conversation. Had not Pangloss been dead, said he, I should combat his system in a victorious manner. God keep me from becoming a Manichean. My mistress taught me to respect the impenetrable veil with which the Deity envelopes his manner of operating upon us. It is perhaps man who precipitates himself into the abyss of misfortunes under which he groans. Of a frugiverous animal he has made himself a carnivorous one. The tribe of savages which we have seen, eat only Jesuits, and do not live upon bad terms among themselves. And those savages, if there be any solitary ones scattered here and there in the woods, only subsisting on acorns and herbs, are, without doubt, still more happy. Society has given birth to the greatest crimes. There are men in society, who are as it were compelled by their condition to wish the death of others. The shipwreck of a vessel, the burning of a house, and the loss of a battle, cause sadness in one part of society, and give joy to another. All is very bad! my dear Cacambo, and there is nothing left for a philosopher, but to cut his throat as gently as possible. You are in the right, says Cacambo : but I perceive a tavern hard by, you must be very thirsty. Come, my old Master! let us drink a cup together, and we will after that continue our philosophical disquisitions.

When they entered the tavern, they saw a company of country lads and lasses dancing in the midst of the yard, to the sound of some wretched instruments. Gaiety and mirth sat on every countenance ; it was a scene worthy the pencil of Watteau. As soon as Candide appeared, a young woman took him by the hand, and intreated him to dance. My pretty Maid, answered Candide, when a person has lost his mistress, found his wife again, and heard that the great Pangloss is dead, he can have little or no inclination to cut capers. Besides, I am to kill myself to-morrow morning ; and you know that a man who has but a few hours to live, ought not

to waste them in dancing. Cacambo, hearing
Candide talk thus, addressed him in these terms :
A thirst for glory has always been the object of
great philosophers. Cato of Utica killed himself, after having taken a sound nap. Socrates
drank the hemlock potion, after discoursing
familiarly with his friends. Many of the English
have blown their brains out with a pistol, after
coming from an entertainment. But I never
yet heard of a great man, who cut his own throat
after a ball. It is for you, my dear Master, that
this honour is reserved. Take my advice, let
us dance our fill, and we will kill ourselves to-
morrow. Have you not remarked, answered
Candide, this young country girl ? Is she not
a very pretty brunette ? She has somewhat very
taking in her countenance, says Cacambo. She
has squeezed my hand, replied the Philosopher.
Did you observe, says Cacambo, that, in the hurry
of the dance, her handkerchief falling aside,
discovered a most beautiful bosom ? I took
particular notice of it. Look you, said Candide,
had I not my heart filled with Miss Zenoida
——The little brunette interrupted him, by
begging him to take one dance with her.
Our hero at length consented, and danced
with the best grace in the world. The
dance finished, he kissed his smart country girl,
and retired to his seat, without calling out the
queen of the ring. Upon this a murmuring
arose ; every one, as well performers as spectators,
appeared greatly incensed and affronted at so

flagrant a piece of disrespect. Candide never dreamed he had been guilty of any fault, and consequently did not attempt to make any reparation. A rude clown came up to him, and gave him a blow with his fist upon the nose. Cacambo returns it to the peasant, with a kick in the belly. In an instant the musical instruments are all broken ; the girls lose their caps ; Candide and Cacambo fight like heroes, but at length are obliged to take to their heels, after a very hearty drubbing.

Every pleasure is poisoned that comes to my lips, said Candide, giving his arm to his friend Cacambo ; I have experienced a great many misfortunes, but I did not expect to be thus beat to a jelly, for dancing with a country girl at her own request.

CHAPTER XVIII

Candide and Cacambo go into an Hospital ; and whom they meet with there.

CACAMBO, and his old master, could hold out no longer, for they were quite dispirited. They began to fall into that sort of malady of the mind, which extinguishes all its faculties : they were ready to sink with despair ; when they perceived an hospital, which was built for the relief of travellers. Cacambo proposed going into it ; Candide followed him. There they met with the usual treatment in such places, in one word they were treated as beggars. In a little time they were cured of their wounds, but they catched the itch. The cure of this malady did not appear to be the work of a day, the idea of which filled the eyes of our philosopher with tears ; and he said, scratching himself, Thou wouldst not let me cut my throat, my dear Cacambo ; thy misplaced counsels have brought me again into disgrace and misfortune ; For should I cut my throat now, it will certainly be said, in the journal of Trevoux, this man was a poor spirited fellow, who killed himself only for having the itch. See what thou hast exposed me to, by the mistaken compassion thou hadst for my fate. Our disasters are not without remedy, answered Cacambo. If you will but please to listen to me, let us settle here, as assistants to the charity ; I understand a little surgery, and I promise you to alleviate and render supportable our wretched condition.—Ah ! says Candide, the devil take all ignorant asses, and especially asses of surgeons, who are so dangerous to mankind. I can never suffer that thou shouldst pretend to be what thou art not : this is a deception, the consequences of which I dread. Besides, if thou didst but conceive how hard it is, after having been Viceroy of a fine province, after having seen one's self rich enough to purchase kingdoms, and after having been the favourite lover of Zenoida, to resolve to serve in quality of assistant in an hospital.—I can conceive all this to be very hard, replied Cacambo ; but I also conceive, that it is very hard to die of hunger. Think, moreover, that the expedient which I propose to you, is perhaps the only one which you can take, to elude the enquiries of that savage Wolhall, and avoid the punishment which he is preparing for you.

One of the brethren of the hospital was passing along as they talked in this manner ; they put some questions to him, to which he gave satisfactory answers : he assured them that the brothers lived well, and enjoyed a reasonable liberty. Candide thereupon determined to follow Cacambo's advice. They put on the dress of the society, which was granted them upon the first application ; and our two miserables undertook to assist others more miserable than themselves.

One day, as Candide was distributing amongst the patients some wretched broth, an old man caught his attention. The visage of this poor wretch was livid, his lips were covered with froth, his eyes half turned in his head, and the image of death strongly imprinted on his lean and fallen cheeks. Poor man, says Candide to him, I pity you, your sufferings must be horrible. They are very great indeed, answered the old man, with a hollow voice like a ghost ; I am told that I am hectical, phthisicky, asthmatic, and poxed to the bone. If that be the case, I muſt be very ill, indeed : yet all does not go so badly, and this gives me comfort. Ah ! says Candide, none but Dr. Pangloss, in a case so deplorable, can maintain the doctrine of Optimism, when all others besides would preach up Pessim—Do not pronounce that abominable word, cried the poor man ; I am the Pangloss you speak of. Wretch that I am, let me die in peace. All is well, all is for the beſt. The effort which he made in pronouncing these words, coſt him the laſt tooth, which he spit up with a quantity of corrupted matter, and expired a very few moments after.

Candide lamented him greatly, for he had a good heart. Notwithſtanding his prejudices, his obſtinate perseverance was a source of reflection to our philosopher ; he often called to mind all his adventures. Cunégonde remained at Copenhagen ; he learned that she exercised there the occupation of a mender of old cloaths, with all possible reputation. He now had quite loſt his taſte for travelling. The faithful Cacambo supported him with his counsels and friendship. Candide did not murmur againſt Providence ; I know, said he, at times, that happiness is not the portion of man : happiness dwells only in the good country of El Dorado, where it is impossible for any one to go.

CHAPTER XIX

New Discoveries.

CANDIDE was not so very unhappy, for he had a true friend. He found in a mongrel valet, what a man may vainly look for in our quarter of the globe. Perhaps nature, which furnishes plants in America, that are proper for the maladies of bodies on our continent has also placed remedies there, for the maladies of our hearts and minds. Possibly there are men in the new world of a quite different conformation of parts from us, who are not slaves to self-intereſt, and are capable of feeling the noble fire of friendship. What an acquisition would it be, if inſtead of bales of indigo and cochineal, all ſtained with blood, some of these men were imported among us ! This sort of traffic would be of vaſt advantage to mankind. Cacambo was of greater value to Candide, than a dozen of red sheep, loaded with the pebbles of El Dorado. Our philosopher began once more to taſte the pleasure of living. It was a comfort to him to attend to the preservation of the human species, and not to be an useless member to society. God gave a blessing to such pure intentions, by giving him, as well as Cacambo, the enjoyment of health. They got rid of the itch, and fulfilled with cheerfulness the painful

functions of their station ; but fortune soon
deprived them of the peaceful security which
they enjoyed. Cunégonde, who had set her
heart upon tormenting her husband, left Copenhagen to follow his footsteps. Chance brought
her to the hospital : she was accompanied by a
man, whom Candide knew to be Baron Thunder-
ten-Tronckh. One may easily imagine what
must have been his surprise. The Baron, who
observed his emotion, addressed him thus ; I
did not tug long at the oar in the Turkish gallies ;
the Jesuits heard of my misfortune, and redeemed
me for the honour of their society. I have made
a journey into Germany, where I received some
assistance from my father's heirs. I omitted
nothing to find my sister ; and having learned at
Constantinople, that she sailed from thence in a
vessel, which was ship-wrecked on the coast of
Denmark, I disguised myself, and took letters of
recommendation to Danish merchants, who have
correspondence with the society : and, in fine,
I found my sister, who still loves you, base and
unworthy as you are of her regard ; and since
you have had the insolence to lie with her, I
consent to the ratification of the marriage, or
rather a new celebration of it, with this express
proviso, that my sister shall give you only her
left hand ; which is very reasonable, since she
has seventy-one quarters, and you have never a
one. Alas ! says Candide, all the quarters of
the world without beauty——Mistress Cunégonde was very ugly, when I had the imprudence

to marry her ; she afterwards recovered her beauty, and another has enjoyed her charms. She is once more grown ugly, and you would have me give her my hand a second time. Not I indeed, my Reverend Father, send her back to her seraglio at Constantinople ; she has done me too much mischief already in this country. Ungrateful man, says Cunégonde, with the most frightful contortions ; be persuaded, and relent in time ; do not provoke the Baron, who is a Priest, to kill us both, to wash out his disgrace with our blood. Dost thou believe me capable of having willingly failed in the fidelity which I owed thee ? What could I do against a man who was my master, and liked my person ? Neither my tears, nor my cries, could have softened his brutal insensibility. Seeing there was nothing to be done, I contrived matters so as to be violated with the least inconveniency possible, and every other woman would have done the same. This is all the crime I have committed, and does not deserve thy indignation. But I know my greatest crime with thee, is having deprived thee of thy mistress ; and yet this action ought to convince thee of my love. Come, my dear Love, if ever I should again become handsome : if ever my bosom should recover its firmness and elasticity ; if—it will be only for thee, my dear Candide. We are no longer in Turkey, and I swear faithfully to thee, never to let myself be ravished again.

The discourse did not make much impression

upon Candide; he desired a few hours to consider what plan he should follow. The Baron granted him two hours; during which time he consulted his friend Cacambo. After having weighed the reasons, *pro* and *con*, they determined to follow the Jesuit and his sister into Germany. They accordingly leave the hospital, and set out together on their travels, not on foot, but on good horses hired by the Baron. They arrive on the frontiers of the kingdom. When a strapping fellow, of a very villainous aspect, surveys our hero with close attention; it is the very man, says he, casting his eyes at the same time upon a little bit of paper he had in his hand. Sir, pardon my curiosity, is not your name Candide? Yes, Sir, so I have always been called. Sir, I flatter myself you are the very same ; you have black eye-brows, well shaped eyes, ears not prominent, of a middling size, and a round face and fresh colour ; to me you plainly appear to be five feet five inches high. Yes, Sir, that is my stature ; but what have you to do with my ears and stature ? Sir, we cannot use too much circumspection in our office. Permit me further to put one single question more to you : Have you not formerly been a servant to Lord Wolhall? Sir, upon my word, answered Candide, quite disconcerted, I cannot conceive what you mean. May be so, Sir, but I know for certain that you are the person whose description has been sent me. Take the trouble then to walk into the guard-house, if you please.—Here, soldiers, take care of this gentleman ; get the black-hole ready, and let the armourer be sent for, to make him a pretty little set of fetters, of about thirty or forty pounds weight. Master Candide, you have a good horse there ; I am in want of a horse of that colour ; I dare say we shall agree about it.

The Baron was afraid to say the horse was his. They carried off poor Candide, and Mistress Cunégonde wept for a whole quarter of an hour. The Jesuit seemed perfectly unconcerned at this catastrophe. I should have been obliged to have killed him, or to have made him marry you over again, says he to his sister ; and, all things considered, what has just happened, is much the best for the honour of our family. Cunégonde departed with her brother, and only the faithful Cacambo remained, who would not forsake his friend.

CHAPTER XX

Consequence of Candide's Misfortune. How he found his Mistress again ; and the Fortune that happened to him.

O Pangloss ! said Candide, what a pity it is you perished so miserably ! You have been witness only to a part of my misfortunes, and I hoped in time to have prevailed on you to forsake the illfounded opinion which you maintained to your laſt breath. No man ever suffered greater calamities than I have done ; but there is not a single individual who has not cursed his exiſtence, as the daughter of Pope Urban warmly expressed herself. What will become of me, my dear Cacambo ? Faith, I cannot tell, said Cacambo ; all I know is, that I will never forsake you. But Miſtress Cunégonde has forsaken me, says Candide. Alas ! a wife is of far less value than a true friend, though he be only a servant.

Candide and Cacambo discoursed thus in the dungeon. From thence they were taken out to be carried back to Copenhagen. It was there that our philosopher was to know his doom : he expeſted it to be dreadful, and our readers, doubtless, expeſt so too ; but Candide was miſtaken, and our readers will be so too. It was at Copenhagen that happiness waited to crown all his sufferings : he was hardly arrived, when he underſtood that Wolhall was dead. This barbarian was lamented by no one, while every body intereſted themselves for Candide. His irons were knocked off, and his liberty was the more flattering, as it procured him the sight of his dear Zenoida. He flew to her with the utmoſt transport ; they were a long time without speaking a word ; but their silence was infinitely expressive. They wept ; they embraced each other ; they attempted to speak, but tears ſtopt

232

their utterance. Cacambo sincerely enjoyed a scene so truly interesting to a sensible being ; he shared in the happiness of his friend, and was almost as much affected as himself. Dear Cacambo ! adorable Zenoida ! cried Candide ; you efface from my heart the deep traces of my misfortunes. Love and friendship are preparing for me future days of serenity and uninterrupted delight. Through what a number of trials have I passed to arrive at this unexpected happiness ! But they are all forgot : dear Zenoida ! I behold you once more ? you love me ; every thing is for the best I am sure, in regard to me ; all is good in nature.

By Wolhall's death, Zenoida was left at her own disposal. The court had given her a pension out of her father's fortune, which had been confiscated ; she shared it with Candide and Cacambo ; she appointed them apartments in her own house, and gave out that she was under great obligations to these two strangers, which inclined her to procure them all the comforts and pleasures of life, and to repair the injustice which fortune had done them. There were some who saw through the motive of her beneficence ; which was no very hard matter to do, considering the great talk her connection with Candide had formerly occasioned. The world in general blamed her, but her conduct was approved by those who knew how to reflect. Zenoida, who set a proper value on the good opinion even of fools, was, nevertheless, too happy to regret the loss of it. The news of the death of Mistress Cunégonde, which was received by the Jesuit Merchants in Copenhagen, procured Zenoida the means of reconciling the minds of all parties in regard to her conduct; she ordered a genealogy to be drawn up for Candide. The author, who was a clever fellow, derived his pedigree from one of the most ancient families in Europe; he even pretended his true name was Canute, which was that of one of the former Kings of Denmark; which appeared very probable, as *dide* into *ute* is not such a great metamorphosis: and Candide, by means of this little change, became a very great Lord. He married Zenoida publicly, and they lived as happily as it is possible to do. Cacambo was their common friend; and Candide would often say, "All is not so well as in El Dorado; but it must be confessed, things do not go on badly."

6|xii|41